TALKING to an AUDIENCE

By VERNON HOWARD

Illustrated by DOUG ANDERSON

STERLING PUBLISHING CO., INC.   **New York**

Talking To An Audience
by Vernon Howard

A SPECIAL INTRODUCTION TO THIS EXCLUSIVE EDITION

I once jokingly commented to Vernon Howard that going from writing children's books to spiritual books made perfect sense, "since we really are just like children." He laughed knowingly. Vernon often said that beneath the smooth veneer of the average adult is a scared little boy or girl. We work hard to hide that fact from ourselves and others, and we avoid anything that might unmask us. Paradoxically, dropping the mask is the key to a new life.

Risking exposure and putting our fears to the test is the one way to see through the frightened child within. That child is just part of the conditioned false nature (ego). It has no power of its own, but believes it has to control everything. It senses its insignificance, but thinks the world revolves around it. We believe the false self is who we really are, and so the painful self-protective process continues.

Vernon Howard had a marvelous message for unhappy men and women: Beyond the false self is the true, higher self. It's there, waiting to guide us, but the false self creates so much noise and distraction, Reality can't get through. To change everything, shake up the false self until it loses its validity in your own eyes. When you just let it go, your life becomes Real — and trouble-free.

The best way to shake up the false self is to make it face its greatest fear of exposure: speaking before an audience. At his spiritual school in Boulder City, Nevada, one of Vernon's primary teaching methods was to have us speak before the group. The lessons we learned from it were invaluable.

At every class students could give a short talk on a truth they had seen. Sometimes Vernon gave an Assigned Topic. This could be both scary and fun. The topic could be anything, and you wouldn't know what it was until you got up to the microphone. The topics could be serious, but often they were hilarious. Some students were more articulate than others, but that didn't matter. The important thing was to make the effort and watch the inner struggle.

Each month we had a banquet where students would gather for "food, fun and entertainment." We provided the entertainment ourselves, which meant many of us had to get "on stage," perhaps for the first time in our lives. One day Vernon invented the 5-second act. These were jokes we would act out, usually in pairs. Many of us turned out to have hidden talents, and were instantly proclaimed as "stars." But again, the real value was in just doing it, and watching what happened (and seeing that most of the awful things our egos feared didn't happen)!

Vernon wanted us to introduce truth principles to others, and so we would go to service organizations, business offices, rest homes — anyplace that requested speakers. Being novice orators, we all still got nervous before our talks. Since our topic was "Success Without Stress," we faced the daunting task of telling others how to eliminate stress, while we ourselves were shaking in our boots! It was an illuminating experience.

During his final year, Vernon had to miss many classes because of his health. A group of students was selected to continue the lectures in his absence. Those students were privileged to receive a very special communication from Vernon about speaking before a group. That private instruction read as follows:

From Vernon Howard:

You must learn to speak from yourself, your natural nature, not from unconscious forces that wrongly speak through you.

To become your natural self be aware of yourself all the time you are speaking. One part of you sees yourself in action while another part is aware of the audience.

While speaking, notice yourself imitating the mannerisms of other speakers who impress you. See and drop imitations, they are not the real you.

Also be aware of your nervousness as you are speaking. Nervousness is the ego-self, your unnatural self that worries if the audience is seeing through you or disapproving of you. If you don't see your nervousness the audience will. Don't be afraid to <u>not</u> be nervous, *and it will fall away. Think deeply about this point.*

When speaking, let Truth be stronger than you are, and all will be well.

Vernon

Trying to find the courage to speak before an audience may be the greatest challenge of your life. But if you do it, you will understand that all your fears were only a creation of your false self. Once you see through what had seemed to be an insurmountable wall, you will know that it was never real at all. Then, for you, nothing will ever be the same.

Dr. Ellen Dickstein
Grants Pass, Oregon

BY
SPECIAL ARRANGEMENT
THE KEN ROBERTS COMPANY and STERLING PUBLISHING COMPANY
present this exclusive edition of the original, out-of-print,
hard cover version first published in 1963.
This word-for-word reproduction is not for sale.

CONTENTS

1. YOU WILL ENJOY TALKING TO AN AUDIENCE! 11
   Your Talks Make You More Valuable . . . Start with This Delightful Rule . . . How to Choose a Topic . . . What Is Your Purpose? . . . Wanted: Exciting Titles! . . . Valuable Points from This Chapter

2. HOW TO PREPARE YOUR TALK THE EASY WAY 20
   Start with a Bang! . . . The Middle Is the Strongest Section . . . How to End Your Talk . . . Important Ideas to Remember

3. ACTIONS THAT MAKE YOU A SKILLFUL SPEAKER 30
   How to Help Yourself . . . Practice with a Friend or Two . . . Classroom Practice Is Valuable . . . How Others Succeed . . . Thoughts to Keep in Mind

4. HOW TO GAIN COURAGE AND SELF-CONFIDENCE 40
   Be a Natural Speaker . . . Take Complete Command of Your Audience . . . How to Build Positive Attitudes . . . A Classroom Plan . . . Summary of Helpful Plans

5. SECRETS FOR GIVING AN EXCITING TALK... 49
Two Ways to Use Anecdotes . . . Let Anecdotes Shed
Light on Your Points . . . Let Anecdotes Provide
Entertainment . . . Anecdotes from History . . . Tell of
Your Own Experiences . . . Use Jokes and Humorous
Stories . . . Local Stories Are Popular . . . Helpful
Points for Your Review

6. LET YOUR WORDS WORK FOR YOU!............... 59
Positive Words Make a Hit! . . . Use Clear Words . . .
Make Your Words Descriptive . . . Paint a Word-
Picture! . . . Your Vocabulary Is Your Treasure . . .
What to Remember about Words

7. YOUR VOICE CAN MAKE YOU ATTRACTIVE... 68
Vary Your Voice . . . How to Warm Up Your Voice
. . . Your Voice and Your Words . . . Reminders from
This Chapter

8. HOW TO LOOK GOOD TO PEOPLE................. 77
Let Your Actions Talk for You . . . The Magic of a
Smile . . . Help Yourself with Gestures . . . Eight Good
Reasons . . . A Summary of Attractive Ideas

9. YOU CAN BE PERSUASIVE............................. 86
Use Facts to Influence Your Audience . . . Statistics
Are Persuasive . . . How to Produce Action . . . Tell
Them Just What Action You Want . . . Show Them the
Rewards of the Action . . . Show Them How to Act
. . . Urge Action At Once . . . Points that Persuade

10. HOW TO MAKE PEOPLE LIKE AND ENJOY YOU 96
What Makes Your Personality Attractive? . . . Speak
with Enthusiasm . . . Be Success-Minded . . . The Most
Valuable Person of All . . . Special Ideas from This
Chapter

11. QUESTION-AND-ANSWER SESSION 105
Fascinating Facts . . . Concentrate on Each Part . . .
Question Session . . . All About Quotations . . . Notes
or Not? . . . Have a Good Time . . . Review of Questions and Answers

12. SPECIAL PLANS FOR PRIZE-WINNING TALKS 114
Visual Display . . . Action! . . . Speech Chart . . . How
to Improve Yourself Quickly . . . Prize-Winning Points
to Review

INDEX... 123

A FRIENDLY NOTE TO YOU, THE READER:

From the author:

At one time a spy was sent to a foreign country on a secret mission. After spying around for a couple of weeks he sent a question back to headquarters. He asked whether his daily reports were of value. Headquarters sent him a reply in secret code. It read:

ESCCSUS!

At first he thought it would be difficult to decode the mysterious message. Then he decided that it might be easier than it looked. He believed that his attention and his energy could solve the mystery. They did! He worked until he had rearranged the letters so that they spelled out:

SUCCESS!

I'd like to invite you to take that same viewpoint as we go through this book together. Learning to talk to an audience is like that spy's secret message. All it really takes is a little of your attention and energy. Then, you may find yourself with that same happy news: SUCCESS!

VERNON HOWARD

Chapter 1

YOU WILL ENJOY TALKING TO AN AUDIENCE!

I'd like to tell you an interesting story about a man who gave a short talk, a talk that changed the history of the world!

This man was called Prince Henry the Navigator. Perhaps you remember him from your history books. In any event, Henry was a Portuguese Prince who lived just before Columbus discovered America. Ever since his youth the Prince had been excited about undiscovered corners of the earth. His enthusiasm for adventure led him to establish a school for sailors and explorers.

At that time there was no way to reach India by ship, and the Prince's ambition was to find a sea route to that distant land. He hoped to send his ships to buy India's spices. So he called his captains and seamen and spoke to them. "I want you to sail hundreds of miles down the coast of Africa. Go farther south than any ship before you. I believe that you will reach the southern tip of Africa. From there you will have clear sailing to India."

The men hesitated. "We don't dare sail that far south," they said. "We've been told that the southern seas boil with fire. We're afraid of those unknown waters."

Their hesitation didn't bother Prince Henry at all. He knew exactly what to do.

He gave a short talk!

He assured his men that they really had nothing to fear. He

displayed maps that showed how it was possible to reach India by sailing south. He reminded them that they would be heroes by being the first to succeed. As for the boiling seas, he explained: "The ocean doesn't really boil. Do you know why the water down there is just a bit warmer? Because the weather itself is warmer!"

What happened as a result of that short talk?

The sailors sailed. They found India!

This newly discovered sea route opened India to all of Europe. All because of a man who knew how to give a short and successful talk!

I wanted to tell you this story at the very start of this book, because it will help you to remember the value of talking to an audience. You may never speak to a crew of frightened sailors. But you do want to talk successfully to your own groups.

YOUR TALKS MAKE YOU MORE VALUABLE

Try talking to an audience!

It can be much more than an enjoyable experience—it may even be an event that brightens your entire personality.

The person who can say a few words to an audience is likely to be called upon wherever he goes. Speaking experiences help one become a leader. They add to your self-confidence. They guide you into saying the right thing at the right time. Talking to an audience trains your mind to think quickly and clearly and wisely.

A test made at one of our colleges proved that students who gave talks were also the most popular. Why is this so? Because your skill in handling an audience is like an overflowing river—it spills over, on to all your other meetings with people. It refreshes your friends.

Audiences like and appreciate the person who delivers a

good talk. A capable speaker *gives* them so much. As we will see in later pages, you can *entertain* your listeners. And you can supply them with needed *information*. You can show them how to *improve* themselves. Everyone likes the speaker who supplies all that!

A young man was asked by a classmate, "Why are you learning to give a talk?"

"Because," the young man answered, "talking is something I do three hundred and sixty-five days a year."

There you have a perfect reason why you should learn to talk well!

START WITH THIS DELIGHTFUL RULE

It is a rule that makes every other rule much easier:
Enjoy yourself!

Those two words are just about the most important in this entire book. Whether preparing or delivering your talk, you should enjoy yourself fully.

John Ruskin, an English author, wrote this happy sentence: "You were made for enjoyment, and the world is filled with things you will enjoy."

That includes talking to an audience!

Have you noticed how much better we do something that we *like* doing? For instance, playing golf. It's not work at all. We cheerfully and enthusiastically swing at the ball. The same with a talk. A happy attitude toward speaking helps you to learn faster, and you make a better talk.

So turn your talk into an adventure. Make it a pleasure. Be light-hearted. One of the nicest things about life is that you can be both light-hearted and serious at the same time. Lots of people don't know this delightful truth. They wrongly think you must be gloomy in order to be serious. You don't. You can be both serious and gay at the same time, as when learning to play a new game. Nothing is more important to remember than this—not only when learning to talk, but with everything else you do.

Besides all this, when you enjoy your speech, your audience enjoys *you*. Talking to an audience is really a fun-filled adventure. So make it one, for both your listeners and yourself!

Anyone can give an interesting talk before others.

How do I know?

Because the rules that show you how are so simple.

If you just finish reading this book, you will learn how to give short talks that last for around five minutes, and if you wish to give longer ones, the very same rules can be used. Just as a short length of railway track has rails and ties, so does a long one. The long track simply has *more* rails and ties. The ideas you will absorb from this book will make it easy for you to give talks of all lengths.

HOW TO CHOOSE A TOPIC

All right. You are ready to go. Where do you start? How do you take that first interesting step?

Begin by asking yourself, "What shall I talk about?"

This is really an easy question to answer. There are *millions* of topics! I have heard interesting speeches on an amazing variety of subjects. Here are just a few: *Chinese history, gold mining, cake making in France, spies, the Mississippi River, earthquakes, space travel, London.*

If your talk is for the classroom, your teacher may assign you a good topic. If you choose your own, it's a good idea to talk about something familiar to you. You will have no trouble here. All of us have wide knowledge on lots of topics. Here are ten examples:

1. Your hobby
2. A holiday trip
3. An experience at home
4. A famous person
5. Your club
6. A sport or game
7. Your pets
8. A book
9. A foreign country
10. Your best-liked school subject

WHAT IS YOUR PURPOSE?

This is the second question. You have your subject, but *why* are you giving this talk to your listeners?

Your *subject* is like a railway train. Your *purpose* is the track that keeps the train on its course.

Here are three different reasons for giving a talk:

To inform: Your purpose may be to inform your audience about a newly-published book. Or you may want to tell them about a school carnival that is being planned. Perhaps your purpose is to inform them of a tourist trip to be taken by bus. An informative kind of talk should include lots of facts presented in an interesting way. One speaker recently was telling his audience about the English language. His talk sparkled with facts. For instance, he informed his listeners that the most popular letter in English is *e*, followed by *t, a, o, n, r, i, s*, in that order.

To persuade: Many talks seek to persuade the audience to do something, to act. The president of a club may wish its members to attend a party. The purpose of a clergyman's sermon may be to persuade his congregation to bring in new members.

Perhaps the reason for your talk is to gain new subscriptions to the school newspaper. Or you may want people to attend the next football game.

The talk to persuade people is a popular one. That is why you will find lots of ideas in this book for being a persuasive speaker.

To entertain: One speaker started his talk like this: "Did you hear about the tiger who entered a café and ordered a bowl of soup? Another customer pulled the waiter aside and whispered, 'Isn't that a bit unusual?' The waiter nodded. 'Sure is. He usually orders a cheese sandwich'."

That was a bright beginning for an entertaining talk. The speaker's subject was *jokes*. His purpose was to make the audience laugh. And that's what he did!

There are other good purposes beside these three. A talk may pay homage to your teacher. Or perhaps you wish to inspire your audience with feelings of patriotism. But start off with these three main purposes—to *inform*, to *persuade*, to *entertain*.

Also, you will find that a talk often has two or three purposes. For instance, a talk that informs people of a bus trip can also be very entertaining. But you should start off with a single purpose and make it the principal reason for your talk.

WANTED: EXCITING TITLES!

Give your talk a title just as soon as you can. It acts like a spotlight to keep your words on your subject. It can even inspire you as you prepare your material. Famous speakers often start their preparations with just a title. Sir Winston Churchill, when he was Prime Minister of Britain, planned his powerful speeches from just a title.

Remember these rules and you will never have title trouble:

1. *Make it simple:* Your title should be easy to understand. People should know what it's all about the first time they hear it. Get right to the point. Use short words and as few as possible.

2. *Make it exciting:* A menu in a café listed *Coconut Cake*. The owner changed it to *Delicious Hawaiian Coconut Cake*. He sold twice as many slices! He succeeded because he turned an ordinary title into an exciting one. Thrill your audience with your title. Appeal to a human emotion, such as curiosity or a desire for adventure.

3. *Make it informative:* A speech entitled *Strange Creatures of the Sea* is both exciting and informative. One young man

announced his title as *How I Captured a Vicious Alligator With My Bare Hands*. But his talk was about the weather. At the end, someone asked him, "I enjoyed your talk, but why did you give it such a meaningless title?" The young man grinned and said, "Oh, I thought it sounded more exciting."

A title should be as interesting as possible, but should also suggest the subject. You need not tell everything in the title—in fact, a touch of mystery is attractive. Just include your topic in some small way.

Magazine articles often carry excellent titles. Here are good ones from the *Reader's Digest:*

Want to Make a Million Dollars?
The Testing of a President
The Art of Saying the Right Thing
How Quick-Witted Are You?
Don't Just Sit There—Reach for the Switch!
What Women Want in the Men They Marry
English—The Language for Everyone?
Be Honest With Yourself!
How to Keep Your Memory Sharp
The Girl Who Wouldn't Give Up

Let's select a subject and build a snappy title for it. Suppose we choose the topic of *chocolate*. We intend telling our audience how chocolate is produced and used. At first we might come up with these three titles:

Chocolate
How Chocolate Is Produced
What I Learned About Chocolate

These three certainly inform us of the topic, but how can we add some excitement? Let's see whether we can come up with a punchy headline. Here we are:

Have a Chocolate!

See the difference? This exciting title pulls the audience into the fun. It's a tasty invitation!

In the next chapter we will have more chocolate, as you will see.

VALUABLE POINTS FROM THIS CHAPTER

1. Remember the success of Prince Henry the Navigator. It proves the value of a short talk.
2. Talking before a group of people brightens your entire personality.
3. All of us should learn to speak well. After all, we talk 365 days a year!
4. Talking to an audience is fun. Make every speech an enjoyable experience.
5. Remember that your audience enjoys a happy and enthusiastic speaker.
6. You can give an interesting talk. Just let the rules work for you.
7. Select a subject of interest to your audience. For your first talks, choose topics familiar to you.
8. Give your talk a clear purpose.
9. Entitle your talk at the very start.
10. Work up a snappy title. A good title is like a magnet—it draws attention!

Chapter 2

HOW TO PREPARE YOUR TALK THE EASY WAY

When General George Washington took command of the American armies, he asked the Continental Congress to supply him with up-to-date maps. The Congress promptly gave him the surveyors and map-makers he needed. It turned out that those maps were worth ten thousand rifles to General Washington.

After you have the topic and title of your talk, and you know your purpose in giving it, what comes next?

A map. You may also call it an outline. It has been said that the best way to avoid unnecessary work is to do things right the first time. Well, your map—your outline—makes everything much easier and more enjoyable.

An outline can be one of the most interesting parts of preparing your talk. It's like writing a story. Just as a story goes from one interesting action to another, so does your outline.

You probably remember the fairy tale of Sleeping Beauty. Here is how it goes, step by step:

1. The King and Queen hold a feast for their daughter, the Princess.

2. A wicked fairy, who was not invited to the banquet, pronounces a curse upon the young Princess.

3. The Princess grows into a beautiful, kindly and lovable young lady.

4. After accidentally hurting her finger while exploring the castle's tower, she falls into a deep sleep.

5. Many brave young Princes try to reach and awaken Sleeping Beauty, but all fail.

6. Finally, a strong and handsome young Prince reaches the tower.

7. He kisses Sleeping Beauty.

8. She awakens, is married to the young Prince and they live happily ever after.

Notice how this outline keeps you interested by going from one strong point to another. That is exactly how your talk can keep your audience listening. Just tell an exciting story by sliding from one exciting point to another.

An outline will help you do this. It organizes your speech into strong and worthwhile points. It helps you to remember those points while talking.

Start by taking a fresh sheet of paper. Give your talk a title. Write it at the top of the page. It need not be the final title you want. Just write down the best one you can think of for now.

Next, write the word *Beginning* below the title. Leave some space and write the word *Middle*. Leave more space and write *Ending*. These are the three main parts of your talk. (They are sometimes called by other names, such as *Introduction*, *Body*, *Conclusion*.) Someone once explained the three sections like this: "First you tell them what you're going to tell them. Then you tell them. Finally, you tell them what you told them."

You are now ready to fill in those empty spaces with important ideas. So write the number *1* under *Beginning*. Next, write a single point that makes a good opening remark. It might look like this:

1. The largest country in the world is Russia.

Or maybe:
 1. Diamonds are a major industry in South Africa.

Write down and number just two or three important ideas for the Beginning. Next, do the same with the Middle. You will want to list about six or seven points for this section, for here is where you will spend most of your talking time. Finally, number and write down a couple of points after Ending.

Here is how our topic of chocolate might look in complete, simple outline:

HAVE A CHOCOLATE!

Beginning:
 1. Chocolate—a tasty treat!
 2. Chocolate, like vanilla and strawberry, is one of the world's three most popular ice creams.

Middle:
 1. Chocolate comes from cacao beans growing on trees.
 2. Most chocolate comes from South America and the West Indies.
 3. It was one of the curiosities that Columbus brought back to Europe after discovering America.
 4. Chocolate is used mainly in sweets, such as candy bars and creams.
 5. It is also used in cakes, pies, puddings, beverages, frostings, syrups, ice cream.
 6. In which form did you last taste chocolate?

Ending:
 1. Chocolate is a fascinating subject—and a tasty treat.
 2. All this talk about chocolate makes you want to rush out and get some!

A short outline like this carries your talk forward smoothly

and easily. Every idea sparks off ideas for other points. Suppose, for example, that you reach point 2 in the Middle. After telling your audience about South America and the West Indies you could show these places on a map. An important idea is like the trunk of a tree. Just as a tree trunk leads to several smaller branches, your major point can lead to a number of smaller but good talking points.

Don't try for a perfect outline the first time. Just write down those ideas that seem important enough to use. Later, you can add or drop various points. The outline will improve itself as you go along.

During your actual talk, you can reduce your outline to a

smaller size. This makes it handy for notes. For instance, the word *tree* might be enough to remind you to talk about the cacao beans. (We'll be discussing the use of notes in Chapter 11.)

START WITH A BANG!

A young man was asked to talk on the topic of band music. He stepped to the platform and started off by giving a long and horrible howl. The audience plugged its ears to the painful shriek. The teacher asked him, "What kind of a beginning was that? I suggested that your start should sound like a swinging note."

"Swinging note?" muttered the puzzled young man. "I thought you said *singing goat*."

It would be safer to say that a good talk should start with some kind of a *bang*. Your very first words should catch attention. You want to draw all eyes and ears your way. Win attention at the very start and you won't have to chase it later on.

Remember, your listeners hope and expect you to give a peppy talk. Prove it with your very first words! Here are four tested ways to start with a bang:

1. *Start dramatically:* A dramatic opening has mystery. Or surprise. Or something unusual. Turn your imagination loose when planning your Beginning. Let it come up with unusual ideas.

Let's think together about *Have a Chocolate!* How about this idea: Step before your audience with these first words: "I want to show you something straight from the jungles of South America." Now you have them curious. They alertly look and listen. They want to see what mysterious object you have. You then take a chocolate bar from your pocket and hold it up.

You solve the mystery. You hold their attention. You have a good and dramatic opening.

2. *Ask a question:* Suppose I ask you, "What famous event in history lasted only twelve seconds?" That catches your attention, doesn't it? You want to know the answer. Well, the first flight of the Wright brothers lasted for just twelve seconds.

Appeal to the curiosity of your audience. Start your talk with a catchy question. Give them the answer. Then roll on to your next point. They will be listening.

3. *Make an exciting statement:* One lecturer who gives talks before businessmen opens his talk like this: "Tonight I'm going to show you in five minutes how to quadruple your earnings." Everyone wants to do *that*—so they sit up and take notice. He then shows them how a certain sales letter, written in five minutes, can return a big profit.

Think of the most exciting point in your talk. Reduce it to a short and snappy statement. You could start like this: "I am going to tell you about an explosion so loud that people heard it three thousand miles away." That could open a talk about the volcanic island of Krakatoa. Back in 1883 this island flew apart in a gigantic explosion.

4. *Open with an anecdote:* A brief story is a perfect way to win attention from the start. Almost any anecdote can be connected with your topic. Chapter 5 shows you how.

Here is an amusing opener used by one speaker:

"A farmer had two horses. He gave one of them to his son Tom, the other to his son Sam. The brothers looked for a way to tell their horses apart. First, they cut the mane of one of the horses, but after a while it grew back. So they had to think of something else. Next, they tied a short piece of rope around the neck of one of the horses, but the rope fell off. So they had to think of another plan. They decided to measure the horses to see whether one was taller than the other. And sure enough, the black horse was an inch taller than the white one."

That anecdote always gets laughter—and attention!

THE MIDDLE IS THE STRONGEST SECTION

The Middle of your talk is where you offer your main points. You carry forward your main purpose. It's the strongest and longest part of your speech. Here is how it compares with the Beginning and Ending.

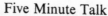

Five Minute Talk

Beginning   Middle   Ending

Here are three steps that make it easy for you to speak all the way through the Middle:

1. *State your point:* For instance, you might say, "Happiness comes to the man who takes responsibility for himself."

2. *Talk about the point:* Offer all sorts of ideas about your point. Discuss the idea that responsibility leads to happiness. Show *why* and *how* self-reliant people are the happiest. Give an example, for instance, show how a sense of responsibility helped General Dwight D. Eisenhower. Prove your statement. Make it exciting. Hammer away at it. Picture your point as a statue. Imagine yourself walking about that statue, seeing it from several different viewpoints. Talk all around it.

3. *Conclude your point:* Finish your idea in just a sentence or two. You might end up like this: "I think you'll agree that personal responsibility builds personal happiness."

Now take your next main point and do the same thing with it.

This simple procedure keeps you stepping easily from one point to another, just as you might step across a stream on solid rocks.

Much of the material in this book applies to the Middle section. For instance, in Chapter 12 you will learn how to give peppy action to your ideas.

HOW TO END YOUR TALK

When you wrap up a birthday present for a friend you don't leave the ribbons untied. You place the gift in the box, wrap it and finish nicely by tying the knots.

That is what the Ending does for your talk. It wraps everything up tightly and neatly.

Your conclusion should contain two major items:

1. A brief review of your main points.
2. A final appeal for action.

1. You can call it a review or a summary, but the idea is to repeat briefly the main points of your talk. It helps your audience to remember them. Here is how one speaker summed up his speech: "Charles B. Knox was a pioneer in the development of gelatine, a health-giving food that is rich in protein. The next time you have gelatine in a salad, a dessert, or a main dish, you will remember this man."

2. Do you want your listeners to act? Are you persuading them to read more books or to enter a school contest? If so, make a final appeal for action. Leave your request ringing in their ears. Chapter 9 helps you to be a persuasive speaker.

A student asked his teacher, "What is the most important thing to do with the end?"

The teacher replied, "End it."

Don't wander beyond the finish. Wrap your talk in a pretty package and present it to your listeners. They will like the gift!

IMPORTANT IDEAS TO REMEMBER

1. Prepare your talk with a simple outline.
2. Think of your outline as a map that guides you easily through your speech.
3. Remember the three main sections: *Beginning, Middle, Ending*.
4. Review the sample outline, *Have a Chocolate!* Let it help you build your own outline.
5. You need not try for a perfect outline the first time. Just get your points down on paper, then improve them gradually.
6. Include two or three sharp points in the Beginning. Catch attention from the very start.

7. Of the four different kinds of openings, choose the one you think best for your talk.
8. Include the strongest points in the Middle.
9. Make the most of each point.
10. End your talk by reviewing your ideas and by appealing for action.

Chapter 3

ACTIONS THAT MAKE YOU A SKILLFUL SPEAKER

When a small boy returned home from his first music lesson his mother asked, "Well, Tommy, how did you do at piano practice?"

"Not so good," he replied, "I have to go back next week."

Whether it's playing the piano or giving a talk, practice is the secret of success. The more experience you have in doing anything, the better you do it. As William Shakespeare declared, "Experience is a jewel."

The teacher of a speech class asked her students to give her some good reasons for practicing. Here are some of the valuable rewards they mentioned:

"Practice sharpens your skill as a speaker."

"It makes every talk a little easier than the one before."

"It builds self-confidence."

"You begin to see how well you can really do things."

"It's fun!"

"Practice teaches you a lot of interesting things you never knew before."

Practice is a bright and sunny experience for you. You might picture it in your mind like a sun sending out rays:

Enjoyment

Poise

Skill

Practice

Knowledge

Enthusiasm

Confidence

There are three main methods for practicing your talk. All three are valuable:

1. By yourself.
2. With a friend or two.
3. In class.

HOW TO HELP YOURSELF

It's always a good idea to practice alone. You can concentrate nicely when by yourself. Make it your purpose to become acquainted with your rising abilities as a speaker. As you have seen, it can be a richly rewarding experience.

Start off by sitting in a chair, as if ready to stand and speak. Next, imagine that you have been introduced as the speaker. Then, rise and walk confidently across an imaginary stage.

Speak a few words to your imaginary audience. You need not give a complete talk at first; your opening words are enough for now. Finally, return to your chair as if your talk is finished—and it was a *good* one!

Do this several times. And take it easy. Don't try to have every detail perfect. It is especially important not to scold yourself for anything you may think is wrong. Simply get yourself into active training. That is all you need to do at this point. Get to know yourself. Take a good look. It is extremely helpful just to *see yourself in action.* Why? Because *self-improvement* comes from *self-understanding.* As you come to know yourself better, you talk better!

Practice also will help you to acquire an easy *habit* of standing up to say a few words. Do you know how a habit is formed? By *repeating* an action. By doing it over and over. You can easily read the words on this page because you have practiced your reading. Well, you can gain a habit by repeatedly standing up and speaking up!

One student practiced at home during the evening by memorizing the first two sentences of his talk. They went like this: "Do you think it best to get all the education you can? One famous man proved that it is." The student then went on to tell the story of Benjamin Franklin. At one time this noted American was discouraged with his studies. But he kept at it. He read books, asked questions, worked at his lessons. Benjamin Franklin turned out to be a great scientist, author and statesman.

Practice this method for yourself. Memorize the first two sentences until they act like a diving board and help you spring off to a confident speech.

Here is another way to get the most from your home training: Write down any of the spots in your talk that seem to need improvement the most. Concentrate on just a few, not more

than three. Next, give each of them your careful attention. Work toward improving them one at a time. Here is how your list might look:

1. Learn more about my subject.
2. Put more excitement into my voice.
3. Remember that I'm talking to a friendly audience.

Oliver Wendell Holmes, the famous American author, once wrote twenty-two inspiring words that should encourage everyone who is learning to talk to an audience. He wrote, "I find the great thing in this world is not so much where we stand, as in what direction we are moving."

You are moving in the right direction when you practice by yourself. Simply do it over and over. That's how you learn to stand before an audience and put yourself over!

PRACTICE WITH A FRIEND OR TWO

A customer bought a used car on Monday. On Friday he drove back into the car lot and asked the salesman, "Remember this car you sold me?"

"Yes," the salesman replied.

"Remember telling me what a great car it was?"

"Yes."

"Well," sighed the customer, "please tell me again. I'm getting discouraged."

You will get encouragement by practicing with a friend who is also learning to speak. You can take turns listening to each other and noticing places for improvement that you might miss alone. One of the fastest ways to make progress in speaking is to get constructive suggestions from someone listening to your training talks.

After each turn, discuss the performance. Offer concrete suggestions for improvement, not vague comments.

Because advice is so important, let's find out how to give and take it.

When you offer advice to another, be sure that you:

1. Make it really helpful.
2. Give it in a kindly manner.
3. Encourage as well as advise.

One way to help another speaker is to point out definite areas calling for improvement. Comment upon a single area at a time, such as his posture or his opening words. Don't tell him, "Your talk was all right, but I guess it could be better." Rather, point out exact places that he can work on. Once he clearly knows what must be done, he can correct things much more swiftly.

All advice should be offered in a kindly and friendly way. This makes your friend *want* to accept your suggestions. All of us appreciate advice when it is given in a pleasant manner. The Golden Rule might be changed a bit for this purpose: "Help others as you would have others help you."

As we have seen, encouragement is helpful. When you tell the speaker about his *good* points, about his *strong* features, you are not only advising but *encouraging*. If the speaker has a sunny smile, tell him so. If she has an ability to tell interesting anecdotes, compliment her for this strong point. If your friend has a pleasing voice, don't hesitate to praise him for it. All of us like and need encouragement. You like it. Your friend likes it.

How about taking advice from others? How can you get the most out of their suggestions? Your best attitude toward helpful criticism is a *happy* attitude. A suggestion from your teacher or a schoolmate should be cheerfully welcomed as an opportunity for self-improvement. With an attitude like that, you are certain to become a better speaker faster.

The giving and taking of advice should be like a game of ball between two friends. Helpful suggestions are tossed back

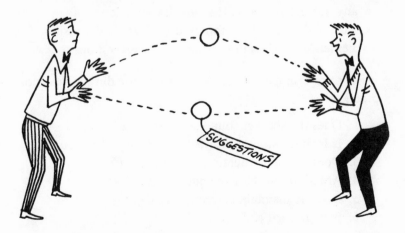

and forth. They are caught and used. And they surely make the game more fun!

CLASSROOM PRACTICE IS VALUABLE

The best thing about classroom training is your teacher's valuable help.

One teacher has an excellent system for getting students off to a fine start as public speakers. Perhaps you can try it in your own classroom:

1. Everyone takes a turn walking to the front of the class. Each states his name in a single sentence, as, "My name is Paul Anderson." The speaker then returns to his seat, and another student goes to the front.

2. On the second round, everyone again steps up to state his name. But he also adds something. He may tell something about his home, as for instance, "I live on High Street, on the west side of town. My home is across the street from a fire station. Fire trucks roll out at all hours of day and night."

3. As a third step, everyone takes a turn at speaking briefly on any subject he likes. His talk lasts no longer than thirty seconds, and each talk is followed by a short discussion. The teacher leads the class in making helpful suggestions.

Here are examples of things to watch for during classroom practice:

1. Does the speaker sound self-confident?
2. Is he interesting to hear?
3. Does he catch attention from the start?
4. Are his words clearly understood?
5. Does he maintain correct posture?
6. Is he relaxed and cheerful?

7. Are his gestures natural?
8. Is he convincing in what he says?
9. Does he avoid a monotonous tone of voice?
10. Is he enthusiastic?
11. Does he look at his audience?
12. Is he in command of his subject?

Make the most of your classroom talks. Listen to advice from your instructor, then apply it. Speak as often as you can. Let your experiences teach you how to perform just a little bit better each time.

HOW OTHERS SUCCEED

This is an excellent place to tell you about two fine organizations. The time may come when you will become a member.

One is called the *Toastmasters International, Inc.* This one is for men who wish to improve themselves as speakers and leaders.

The other is the *International Toastmistress Clubs, Inc.* This club helps women develop their speaking talents and shows them how to take charge of meetings.

They have hundreds of clubs throughout the United States. Perhaps your city or town has one. Clubs are also organized in other nations, including England, Australia and Japan.

In this chapter we've been discussing your *training* as a speaker. And training is where these two clubs are especially helpful to their members. Thousands of people have become speakers—and better speakers—in the club meetings. Men and women find lots of opportunity for on-their-feet experience. That is how they increase both their confidence and skill.

I wanted to tell you about these two fine organizations for a definite reason: It proves that tens of thousands of people know the value of being a good public speaker. They realize the rich rewards it gives to others and to themselves.

Do you know how Thomas A. Edison became one of the most famous inventors of all time?

He *practiced* inventing. In other words, he kept at it.

Do you know why Henry Ford became one of the world's great industrialists?

He *trained* himself constantly. In other words, he kept on improving things.

Do you know how you can become a successful speaker?

By *practicing* your speech-making. In other words, by cheerfully speaking again and again.

So do it!

THOUGHTS TO KEEP IN MIND

1. Enjoy your practice periods.
2. Practice by yourself, with a friend, and in class. Make the most of each method.
3. Remember, the more you repeat an action, the more habitual it becomes. Build good speech habits.
4. Concentrate on those places where you need improvement the most.
5. When you check another's speech, let your advice be helpful and encouraging.
6. After your practice talk, welcome all helpful suggestions. The easy way to improve yourself is to have a mind like a good hotel—open all the time!
7. Take guidance from your teacher.
8. One of the greatest of life's pleasures is seeing how much better you can do something. Make each talk a little better than the one before.
9. Hundreds of years ago a wise man named Publilius declared, "Practice is the best of all instructors." It's just as true today!

Chapter 4

HOW TO GAIN COURAGE AND SELF-CONFIDENCE

I remember reading an exciting adventure story about a soldier named Burt. During a battle he was captured by the enemy and sent to a prison camp. Every night for three weeks he dug away at a tunnel beneath the camp wall. Finally, on an ink-black night, he crawled through the tunnel and escaped into nearby woods. For the next several days he dodged the enemy patrols sent out to catch him. Once they came so close to his hiding place that he could hear them breathing.

As he ran out of the woods he found himself near a school, so he decided to go in and ask a teacher for directions. The teacher looked at his old clothes and mistook him for a camp director who was coming to lecture. The soldier was about to correct her when he saw a squad of enemy soldiers approaching. So he went along with the teacher. She led him to a hall with a lecture platform where he was enthusiastically introduced by the principal who cheerfully described him as "a forestry expert who will tell us all about the wonders of nature."

Burt didn't know much about the wonders of nature. But he *was* a self-confident man. He simply stepped up and talked! He told of the wonderful ways in which trees serve the world. He noted that trees supply lumber, bear fruit, give shade, provide beauty, and so on.

It wasn't exactly a prize-winning speech, but it delighted everyone. His easy-going boldness kept the room chuckling.

Even his mistakes were fun. As he finished, the class applauded enthusiastically.

The soldier waved a cheery good-by and slipped out of a side door. Then he kept running until he reached the safety of his own army.

That soldier's amusing adventure shows us the value of self-confidence:

It helps you to think on your feet.
It gives you control over your hearers.
It keeps you calm and relaxed.
It gives your audience confidence in you.
It turns your imagination loose.
It makes you feel good!

A young man in a speech class remarked to me, "If I had more courage and confidence, I know that everything else would be much easier."

That's right. Everything is smoother for the person in charge of himself.

That young man then asked, "How can I build my self-confidence?"

That is what we will now find out.

BE A NATURAL SPEAKER

A sparrow wings across the sky with the greatest of ease. A salmon swims effortlessly through the ocean waters. A deer races lightly and smoothly across the meadow.

None of them has any trouble moving along with full confidence and skill. Why? Because they are doing things naturally, the way nature intended.

You can be just as wise. Simply make it a point to drop all

unnecessary effort and do things the natural way, the easy way! You may not fully realize it, but nature has given you a powerful confidence in your own abilities. Your confidence springs from being your natural self. Naturalness and courage are like two sides of a coin—if you have one, you also have the other.

We will soon see how this connects with your self-assurance as you stand before an audience.

But first I want to tell you something about the human mind and how it works. Have you noticed that whenever you talk with a friend you speak easily, without effort or strain? When you walk down the street, you speak confidently, freely, and always think of something to say. You're neither scared nor hesitant. Your words pour out like water over a falls. You're completely confident.

Now why is this? Why is everything so smooth and comfortable? It's because you are being yourself, because you are not trying to make an impression on your friend. You are talking simply and naturally.

You are able to think of words to say when you don't try to *force*, any more than you have to force yourself to walk.

Now, if you will carry this same kind of naturalness into

your speaking you will be just as self-assured. Remember you are not only talking *to* your audience, but *with* them. Speak to them as you would speak with friends, for that is exactly what they are. The best kind of talk sounds something like a conversation. The only difference is that your talk is organized conversation. This phrase, *organized conversation*, is a good one to remember.

You need not strain to be a clever speaker. You don't have to work at making your audience like you. Just give a simple and honest talk. An audience likes a simple, natural and pleasant speaker.

Be sincere. Be yourself. These are the personal qualities that audiences enjoy.

Oh, yes, when you speak *naturally*, you are certain to speak *confidently*.

TAKE COMPLETE COMMAND OF YOUR AUDIENCE

If you will remember this golden rule, you will quickly build yourself into a strong speaker.

How does this build confidence in yourself? We will discover that in a moment. First, I want to give you a hint to remember the importance of taking charge.

Imagine yourself as the driver of a sight-seeing bus loaded with eager passengers. How would you act? Why, you'd take complete command, of course. First you would assure the riders that you are about to begin an enjoyable adventure together. You would make them feel that you are a skillful and confident guide. And then you would actually drive them to the mountains and woods and valleys. Your leadership is their pleasure.

To take command you must speak and act as if you are in charge of the situation. And the truth is, you *are* in charge.

The speaker is the leader. The people in the audience recognize the speaker as the person in charge. By coming to hear you speak they have invited you to control their time and attention for the next several minutes. This is a fine opportunity for you to build your powers of leadership.

Remember, your audience is eager to listen to you. The more you take charge the more they can relax and enjoy themselves. Every audience will admire the speaker who takes the responsibility for leading them.

Now let's see how that very same leadership builds your own self-certainty.

William James, the famous psychologist, helped thousands of people become courageous individuals. Here is how he advised them: "The more you do something, the better you do it. Never mind whether or not you have courage to do a new task— just do it. Your courage will rise as surely as the morning sun."

You need to start taking charge of your listeners by catching their attention with your very first words. Speak right up as if you know exactly what you are talking about—for you really do! Then continue that way for the rest of the talk.

Never act or speak in an apologetic manner. Don't tell your audience that you consider yourself a poor speaker. If you make a mistake, correct it in any way you can, then go on. Do not be embarrassed by anything you do. And especially do not scold yourself if you make a blunder. You are a human being. When you make mistakes you *prove* that you are human —just like everyone else!

Recently, one young lady used these ideas. She told me afterwards, "You know, Mr. Howard, it really works. The instant I spoke up with confidence, I really *was* confident!"

It can work for you, too. Remember, when you *take* charge, you *are* in charge.

HOW TO BUILD POSITIVE ATTITUDES

Here is a method you can use when practicing alone:

Poke your finger at any page of this book. Let it land anywhere. Find the noun that is nearest your fingertip. It can be the name of a person, a place, or thing. Examples: *President, soldier, wood, sea, bus, chocolate.*

Have it? All right. Talk!

Speak up. Never mind whether or not you know anything about the topic. Just turn your imagination loose and start talking. Have fun. Relax. Talk any way you like.

You'll be surprised how easily you can think of things to say about your subject. The secret is to let yourself go. Let things happen. Ideas come rapidly to the mind that doesn't try too hard. So don't strain yourself. Just talk easily.

You may never have heard of the Minnesota Mining and Manufacturing Company, but at one time this company decided to offer a new and unusual product to the public. They called it Scotch Brand cellophane tape. The firm believed that people would like to use this new tape for sealing packages. So they placed it on sale.

Surprisingly, thousands of letters poured in to the company. People told of dozens of different uses. It mended torn papers. It was handy for sealing open jars. It kept announcements attached to bulletin boards. Good ideas came from all over the world.

That's how it can be with you, too. Start with a single idea—your topic. Turn it loose. Don't wonder how to start—just start anywhere. You don't have to be perfect. The purpose is to stretch your mental muscles. Just let yourself go and you'll go right ahead!

A CLASSROOM PLAN

For a second method (used by many teachers of public speaking), you will play a game in the classroom.

The teacher assigns everyone a subject. Or, she can allow students to choose their own. There is just one rule about the topic—it must be funny! Here are ten titles that give you the idea:

1. Why Cheese Tastes Better on Monday
2. What Happened When I Sang a Song
3. You Can Learn to Like Leopards
4. What You Should Do With a Whistle
5. Where to Find Red-Headed Giants
6. How I Swam the Atlantic Ocean
7. Why You Should Live in a Cave
8. Six Ways to Slide Down a Mountain
9. How to Look Intelligent
10. The First Time I Tasted Purple Cabbage

Each speaker takes a turn with his subject. He talks as long as he can. Here is how someone could go along with *Why Cheese Tastes Better on Monday:*

"Ladies and gentlemen, you are in for a shock. Please prepare yourself. I'm sure that many of you believe that cheese tastes the same any day. Others think that there is nothing like Thursday cheese. Some say never on Sunday. Some say cheese only when taking a snapshot. There may even be a few of you who cling to the old-fashioned idea that Tuesday is the cheesiest day of all. The truth is that cheese tastes better on Monday. I'm not content merely to make that statement. I stand ready to *prove* it!

"First of all, let's take a look at Monday. It's the first day

of the week. Oh, you think Sunday is the first day because it's that way on the calendar? You must be a Saturday cheese person. Anyway, Monday is the first *school* day. No disagreement there?

"Now, suppose you carry a cheese sandwich to school on Monday. You won't wait till Tuesday to eat it, will you? You would have a pretty stale hunk of green cheese, wouldn't you? So, you eat it on Monday! Are you beginning to see why cheese tastes better on Monday?"

Notice that this speaker used all the ideas he could dream up quickly on every word of his subject—cheese, taste and the day of the week. He talked about things he knew, and he talked *to* his audience, just as in a conversation. This exercise is good for a classroom contest. First prize can go to the best speaker—or the funniest!

Best of all, the practice is good for building courage and self-confidence—yours.

SUMMARY OF HELPFUL PLANS

1. Speak in a natural manner. Give a simple and sincere talk.
2. Talk to your listeners just as you talk with friends. Your hearers *are* your friends!
3. Be a leader. Take charge of your audience from the very start.
4. Don't apologize for mistakes. Correct them as best you can, then continue.
5. Practice alone by selecting a single word from this book. Stretch your abilities by talking about it.
6. For classroom fun, talk about an odd subject. It's fun and profit for everyone.
7. Practice constantly at building your self-confidence. It will rise just as surely as the sun!

Chapter 5

SECRETS FOR GIVING AN EXCITING TALK

Like to hear a mystery story? All of us do! I'll tell you one that Navy men consider the most baffling riddle ever tossed up by the sea.

At three o'clock in the afternoon of a clear December day, Captain Morehouse was strolling the deck of his sailing ship, the *Dei Gratia*. The voyage had proceeded to a point about one hundred miles off the coast of Portugal.

Captain Morehouse glanced across the calm sea to notice a passing ship. The stranger appeared to be just another two-masted trading vessel on her way to some distant port.

At least that's the way it looked at first to Captain Morehouse. There was nothing unusual about the other vessel.

Then he raised his binoculars.

And so began the celebrated mystery of the Phantom Ship, otherwise known as the *Mary Celeste*.

Captain Morehouse stared hard at the stranger. It was curious the way she chopped aimlessly across the water, first one direction, then another. It was also strange that the *Mary Celeste* failed to answer signals from the *Dei Gratia*.

The captain shouted a command. The *Dei Gratia* sped toward the strange vessel. As he pulled alongside, Captain Morehouse ordered a boat lowered.

On the deck of the Phantom Ship the captain glanced left and right. He frowned in bewilderment. No sign of life. The only sound was the soft slap of sail. The captain ordered his crew to search below deck. Nothing. No one, Empty cabins. Silence, except for the creak of timber straining with the rolling sea.

Back on deck, there was a weird moment, as everyone paused to stare at each other.

Captain Morehouse noted that the *Mary Celeste* was in perfect shape. There was no damage anywhere. Food and supplies were stored in abundance. The sails were set properly. There was no sign at all of disaster or violence.

The last entry in the ship's log was dated ten days before. It gave the vessel's position as some five hundred miles away from its present position.

What had happened to the captain and crew of the *Mary Celeste?* Where had they gone? And *why?*

The only people who knew the answer were not to be found.

What happened to the Phantom Ship?

That is still an unanswered question.

TWO WAYS TO USE ANECDOTES

What has a story to do with a talk? Just about everything! That's why we started this chapter with the mystery of the *Mary Celeste*. It's the perfect type of story to brighten your talk.

Everyone likes a good story, including, of course, the people in your audience. Notice how the speakers you like best make their talks sparkle with stories.

A Los Angeles teacher makes practical use of stories in her speech classes. At the start of the term each student gives a story-telling talk, made up of two or three anecdotes, or a single longer story. It lasts no longer than a few minutes. The plan works out nicely. Since anyone can tell a story fairly well when talking with friends, he can also do the same thing easily before the class. This starts the group off with a wave of confidence.

In what ways do anecdotes help a talk? They serve two main purposes. They are helpful when you want to:

Illustrate a point.
Add entertainment and renew interest.

Let's see how they accomplish these purposes.

1. LET ANECDOTES SHED LIGHT ON YOUR POINTS

Use a story to illustrate your point. You can make it clearer with an anecdote, and help your hearers understand your ideas. Suppose your talk included this statement:

"One of the best ways to succeed at anything is to persist, to keep trying."

To clarify that point, you can tell a story about it. Here is how you might slide naturally into your illustration:

"Clara Barton, the founder of the American Red Cross, once proved that persistence can overcome obstacles. During the Civil War she sought permission to go to the front lines as a nurse, but the War Department ignored her request. She then appealed to several prominent people, including the Governor of Massachusetts. It took lots of time and energy, but no permission was given. Still, Clara Barton kept trying. Finally, the Surgeon General of the Union Army granted her a pass. The courageous woman promptly headed for the scenes of battle. Later, President Lincoln and the entire nation were grateful that Clara Barton had been persistent, for she saved hundreds of lives on the battlefield."

See how that short story proves your point—and makes it clearer?

2. LET ANECDOTES PROVIDE ENTERTAINMENT

Even when your talk is a serious one you can drop in entertaining stories now and then. They keep your subject interesting. But be sure to use tales connected with your main subject or with a particular point. Read the following example, then I'll tell you how it was used in an actual talk.

"Some years ago a sailor was visiting a friend of his in Boston. Her name was Susan Stavers. One evening Susan served the seaman a dish of tapioca pudding. He glanced down at the rough and lumpy dessert, then looked up at Susan, puzzled.

'Is it all right?' Susan worriedly asked.

'Well,' he replied, 'I *have* seen better tapioca.'

'Oh!' she indignantly shot back. 'So you've seen better pudding than mine!'

He gave her a kindly nod. 'I really have, Susan.'

'And I suppose you can improve it!'

'Sure. Look, Susan, just grind it up. Before you cook the tapioca, run it through your coffee grinder.'

That's just what Susan did. The tapioca came out so smooth and tasty that all of her guests asked for more. The demand was so great that she put it up in packages. She soon had dozens of eager customers for her new kind of tapioca pudding.

The next time you see *Minute Tapioca* on your grocery shelves, you'll know how it got its start."

That true story was included in a talk given by the teacher of a class in cooking.

There is no end to the number of interesting anecdotes that are ready for your use. The library contains enough tales to keep you talking for years! Search around for books and magazines offering the best material. Also, keep your eyes open for interesting stories in the newspapers. Your audience will like

to hear of exciting events happening all round the world. Tell about the new kinds of space ships that will soon be ready to zoom off to the moon.

Stories are like an endless supply of money in the bank. You can draw out as much as you like and still be rich! Of the many different kinds of usable material, here are four:

ANECDOTES FROM HISTORY

Katherine Lee Bates, a teacher, once visited Pike's Peak in Colorado. She was so inspired by the beautiful view that she wrote a poem about it. In another part of the country a man named Samuel A. Ward composed a pleasurable melody. That poem and that melody were combined. They produced the lovely patriotic song, *America the Beautiful.*

This historical story can be used to show how cooperation between people produces harmonious results.

History supplies thousands of fascinating adventures that pack excitement into your talk. Here is one told by a recent speaker:

"At one time in history there was no such thing as cake. At least not the kind of cake we know today. Ancient peoples had to settle for different kinds of breads. They baked them from wheat, oats and rye. They were healthful, but you can't use bread for a sweet dessert. That was how it was for hundreds of years. Then, some English cooks began experimenting with their bread-making. They added tasty items, such as sugar and nuts and raisins. Those sweet ingredients magically turned bread into cake. That made the English people very happy. And everyone else ever since!"

TELL OF YOUR OWN EXPERIENCES

You have had all sorts of personal experiences and adventures. Some are just right for your talk. Select those that your audience can picture in imagination. For instance, you might tell about getting lost in the woods, and finally finding your way back to camp. Your listeners would enjoy hearing how you accomplished something, like learning to skate—after a dozen falls!

One clever girl found a way to add an *extra* story to her personal adventure. Her talk started with her trip to the Columbia River in the state of Washington. After a couple of minutes she mentioned seeing the salmon jump out of the water to leap up the smaller falls. She then told her audience:

"It puzzled me how salmon could jump as *high* as all that. No one I asked seemed to know how they did it. So the first thing I did when we got home was to visit the library. I read up on salmon—and discovered what made them such high jumpers. There is usually a deep pool directly below a fall. The salmon swim to the very bottom of it. Then, with one mighty upward dash they hit the surface. The force of that rush sends them sky high."

Think of an adventure that you've had. Choose the incidents that are the most interesting or exciting or funny. String them together into a talk. Let your audience enjoy your adventure!

USE JOKES AND HUMOROUS STORIES

Anything that brings a laugh or smile to your audience is always welcome. Almost all kinds of talks need refreshing jokes. It's easy to connect a humorous story or joke to the idea you want to get over.

Ruth: What do you do when you see a very beautiful girl?

Lois: Oh, I admire her for awhile and then I set down the mirror.

How could that connect with a talk? Well, you can use it

to point out this lesson: While we should all have self-confidence, watch out for vanity!

Here are three more. See whether you can find ways to use them:

Timmie: Mommy, why does it rain?
Mother: To make trees and flowers grow.
Timmie: Then why does it rain on the pavement?

Dad: Benny, are you tossing stones into the goldfish bowl?
Son: No, but I'm coming close.

Norman: I can tell you the score of the ball game before it starts.
Harold: What is it?
Norman: Nothing to nothing.

LOCAL STORIES ARE POPULAR

Your own city is full of stories waiting to be told. People like to hear about local people and places. Your anecdote could tell about a well-known person in the community. It might mention a familiar park or a statue in that park. You can build a lively story around a local event, such as a parade or carnival. Every community has something special about it.

Here is a fascinating local story told by a speaker in New York City:

"Back in the year 1780 the British frigate *H.M.S. Hussar* sailed into Long Island Sound. She carried a cargo of gold and silver. Her rich shipment was intended to pay the salaries of British soldiers who were then battling the Americans in the Revolution. While cruising in the East River, the *Hussar* struck a submerged rock and sank at once. She rested in waters so shallow that for years afterward her masts could be seen

above the water. Both American and British experts tried to recover the wealthy cargo. But tricky currents beat back their efforts.

"The *H.M.S. Hussar* is still there, right in the East River, in the very middle of New York City! Perhaps some day some of the millions of people who pass that treasure every day will discover a way to recover it."

Stories are exciting to your audience, and they are helpful to you. There you have two perfect reasons for using them!

HELPFUL POINTS FOR YOUR REVIEW

1. Anecdotes can be helpful in your talk. More than that, they are fun!
2. Practice telling stories.
3. Use anecdotes to illustrate important points.
4. Make your stories informative, as well as entertaining.
5. Keep your eyes open for good stories. They are like birds coming to a garden—they fly in from all directions!

6. Stories from history are always popular.
7. Don't hesitate to describe your personal adventures.
8. Refresh your audience with humorous stories. Practice at connecting jokes with your points.
9. Entertain with anecdotes about your community.
10. Regardless of the kind of talk you give, use exciting stories!

Chapter 6

LET YOUR WORDS WORK FOR YOU!

What makes a talk?

Words!

A talk consists of inspiring words, informative words, persuasive words, and many other kinds of words. But we should realize something else about words: that they can *work* for us.

A college boy had heard that Mark Twain, the famous author, was highly paid for his writings. So he wrote to him:

Dear Mr. Twain:

I understand that you are paid $1 for each word you write. I'm mailing you a one-dollar bill. Please send me one of your words.

Mark Twain replied, "Thanks!"

In a different way, you can make words work for you. They are your helpful servants, in a talk before an audience or in friendly conversation. So let's find ways to make words and sentences work. But before we start, I want to give you an encouraging thought: You need not try to understand everything the first time. Take it easy and grasp the ideas as best you can at the start. Later, you can add to your understanding by reviewing these pages.

There are dozens of things you can learn about words (enough to fill this entire book!), but we will concentrate on just a few:

1. The value of positive words.
2. Why you should be clear.
3. How to use descriptive phrases.
4. A method for speaking picturesquely.
5. Ideas for building your vocabulary.

POSITIVE WORDS MAKE A HIT!

The speaker who goes over with a smash is the speaker who uses positive words. What is a positive word? A word that gives listeners a "plus" feeling—a good warm feeling. It can be a word of courtesy. Or one extending a friendly invitation. Or perhaps one that excites your audience.

Positive words are strong, bright and kind.

After a classroom contest, the teachers examined the winning talks. They were a lot alike in one way—all were sprinkled with positive words and phrases. Here are some of the sentences that made the audience feel good:

"Your attention is appreciated."

"Please relax and enjoy yourself."

"I'd like to have your opinion."

"You're invited to take part."

"Everyone can brighten his personality."

"Look at this fascinating exhibit."

"Please feel free to ask questions."

"Let's have a good time with this subject."

We can better understand positive words by examining their opposites—negative words. Negative phrases are the gloomy and complaining ones. Saying something sharply critical about someone is negative. So is the apologetic remark, "I guess I'm not making myself clear." Quite often a good talk is weakened by unnecessary words like these. All you have to do with negative words is avoid them!

I want to give you an extra special reason for loading your talk with strong and happy words:

For many years psychologists have known an interesting truth about the words you speak. The *kind* of words you use in daily conversation helps make you the person you are! If you speak gloomily, you talk yourself right into a sad mood. But cheery and courageous words make you feel fine!

So you have two good reasons for including the one kind of words and for avoiding the other kind:

1. It makes your hearers feel good.

2. It makes *you* happy!

You may ask, "How can I make sure that my talk sparkles with positive words?"

It's easy.

Take a positive attitude toward *everything* about your speech. Be glad you're giving it. See it as a happy opportunity for self-improvement. Enjoy that friendly audience. A stream sparkles merrily down the mountainside because that is its natural way. When you are inwardly merry, your words likewise sparkle with natural merriment.

USE CLEAR WORDS

Larry and Harry were standing on the shore of a lake. Larry threw a stick far out into the water. His collie promptly ran out *on top* of the water to pick up the stick and bring it back. Three more times Larry tossed the stick. Each time the frisky collie returned it by running *on top* of the lake.

"Well," Larry proudly remarked, "what do you think of my dog?"

"Too bad," replied Harry, as he shook his head, "that he can't swim."

Remember, some of your listeners may be like Harry. They may miss the point entirely. That is why you need to make your words as clear as a whistle.

Use simple words, easy-to-understand ones. Make sure your words are clear. Don't use a big word when a little one will serve. Don't try to be a great speaker. Be a simple one.

Be just as clear with your strings of words, with your *sentences*.

Don't say, "My primary inclination regarding the clustered fruit of the vine is consistently positive."

Say, "I like grapes."

During World War I a French general had an important message to send to headquarters. The note was gently attached to the leg of a pigeon. The bird flew off. An hour later the message reached Paris. What made everything go so smoothly? The pigeon flew straight for his destination. No stalling, no wandering. It got right to the point!

That's a helpful story to remember. Keep reminding yourself of the purpose—or destination—of your talk. Use words that carry important messages. Whatever your aim may be, keep heading toward it all the time.

Do this, and your listeners will get the message!

MAKE YOUR WORDS DESCRIPTIVE

Little Willie wrote a sentence on the blackboard. It read:

The train went through the tunnel.

His teacher suggested that he rewrite it: "Put some excitement into your sentence. Use descriptive words," she advised. So Willie tried again, like this:

The train crashed, smashed, plunged, rattled, roared, thundered, slammed, cracked, zoomed, banged, boomed through the tunnel!

Willie had the right idea all right. It was just that he had too many ideas!

This brings us to a clever way to make your talk more descriptive: Use synonyms.

A synonym is a word meaning the same thing as another

word. Or, it can mean *nearly* the same thing. Synonyms are like different varieties of apples in a fruit stand, like the *Jonathan*, *Delicious*, and *Rome Beauty*. All are apples, but each has its own special tint and taste. The same with synonyms. They express the same idea but in different ways.

Here is how to enjoy yourself while learning about synonyms. Take a sheet of paper and write down the following sentences:

Jerry *walked* across the room.
Helen is a *beautiful* girl.
Walter proved his *strong* muscles.

Now, see how many synonyms you can find for *walked*, *beautiful*, *strong*. Make a list for each. Just write down all the words you can think of that mean the same or nearly the same. If you wish, you can do this now, before you read further.

Here are ten synonyms for each. (See how many you got.)

Walked: marched, paced, tramped, strolled, sauntered, rambled, staggered, ambled, wandered, stepped.

Beautiful: attractive, pretty, gorgeous, lovely, glamorous, graceful, sparkling, refined, elegant, exquisite.

Strong: powerful, mighty, muscular, forceful, hardy, solid, firm, sturdy, tough, healthy.

As part of your speech improvement, use a variety of words. Once you select a word, look it over. See whether you can replace it with a synonym that is stronger or more exciting.

PAINT A WORD-PICTURE!

Descriptive words are like paints. A talented artist can paint beautiful pictures with mixtures of red, yellow, blue, and you can paint descriptive word-pictures for your audience. They literally make your talk picturesque.

You are about to read parts of two popular poems. See whether you can discover the phrases that make them especially exciting:

Twinkle, twinkle, little star,
How I wonder what you are;
Up above the world so high,
Like a diamond in the sky.

Notice the clear picture you get from the line *Like a diamond in the sky.* It helps your mind to "see" that star as it sparkles like a diamond!

Here is the other, from Henry Wadsworth Longfellow's pleasant poem, *The Day is Done:*

And the night shall be filled with music,
    And the cares, that infest the day,
Shall fold their tents, like the Arabs,
    And as silently steal away.

Look at the line *Shall fold their tents, like the Arabs.* You can ·picture those Arabs moving around, can't you?

These "like" phrases are called similes, because they show similarities between different objects or ideas. Here are three more similes:

They ran like rabbits.
He laughed like a clown
She's as graceful as a deer.

Add a few similes of your own to your talks. They can be either serious or funny. Think of them as word-pictures. That's how your audience sees them!

YOUR VOCABULARY IS YOUR TREASURE

Discovering new words is as much fun as a treasure hunt. In fact it *is* a search for valuable treasure. The more words you know and use, the wealthier you are. When you speak with a variety of phrases you enrich your conversations, you write finer letters and school compositions. And your talk to an audience sparkles like silver when you choose interesting words.

There are more than 600,000 words in the English language. You are not expected to use that many. In fact, you will need only a handful for your everyday speech. But you should know the meaning of as many words as possible. It helps you to get more out of your reading and listening.

Whenever you run across a new word, march straight for the dictionary. Or, if you can't do that, write it down in a notebook and look it up later. Think of a new word as a fascinating puzzle to solve. Then solve it. From that day on you are in command of that word!

Many teachers use this interesting plan for increasing vocabularies:

Each student brings to class a new word he has just discovered, and gives a short talk about it. First, he must pronounce it correctly. Then, he explains its meaning. This speech game builds vocabulary quickly.

Of course words alone will not enable you to talk to an audience successfully, but you can't learn everything overnight either. Make up your mind that you will increase your vocabulary a little bit each day, because this is one of the ways to become a wealthier person.

WHAT TO REMEMBER ABOUT WORDS

1. Remember the value of your words.
2. Let them work for you. Make your words your helpful servants.
3. Use positive phrases. They win your audience and make you feel better.
4. Avoid unhappy and gloomy sentences.
5. Take a cheerful viewpoint toward your talk.
6. Be clear in everything you say.
7. To get over your point, get right to the point.
8. Use a pleasing variety of words. Get the habit of expressing yourself in different ways.
9. Remember that words are like paints. Add some picturesque similes to your talk.
10. Build your vocabulary constantly. Go on a treasure hunt for new and valuable words.

Chapter 7

YOUR VOICE CAN MAKE YOU ATTRACTIVE

Like to make an interesting experiment? If you are in a place where you can speak out loud, you can try it right now. If you are in a class or library, try it later.

Here is a short sentence to speak. As you say it, concentrate on hearing your own voice. Listen carefully to how it sounds.

"When I speak, this is how my voice sounds."

What did you hear? How did it sound? Was it a deep voice or a high one? Were the words spoken clearly? Did your voice have energy and enthusiasm?

Repeat the sentence. Listen again. Did you speak slowly or did your words tumble out swiftly? Did your voice sound strong and confident, or was it somewhat timid and hesitant?

Say the sentence out loud three or four times. Each time, make a fresh examination. This can be a very amusing experience. One girl who tried it laughed and said, "It's like hearing my own voice for the very first time!" Your voice is such a commonplace thing that you rarely take time to notice it.

This experiment is more than amusing. It has practical value.

The purpose is to get you *acquainted* with your own voice, make you aware of how it actually sounds. That is the first step toward a more attractive voice.

Perhaps you have noticed how this idea of *acquaintance* helps you in other parts of your life, in your friendships, for example.

The better you know your friends, the more easily you talk and act together. It's the same with your voice—you want to discover everything you can about using it, so that you can talk better and develop a voice that pleases both your audience and you.

How important is your voice to your audience?

A test made in Chicago showed some astounding results. Taking turns, five people talked on the telephone with a total stranger. Each conversed with him for a couple of minutes. Then, the five people were asked to give their opinions of the stranger, tell how he appeared to them, judged only by his voice.

The stranger was described in many different ways. The opinion of one listener was often the exact opposite of another listener. For instance, one woman thought that the stranger was somewhat nervous, but another woman described him as perfectly calm. Other descriptions of the stranger were: *pleasant, a businessman, tall, wealthy, blue eyes, energetic, polite, probably dressed in a blue suit*. One listener even got the impression that he liked pickles!

That test shows how people form opinions just by hearing a voice. As speakers, we want to remember that!

VARY YOUR VOICE

Once upon a time there was a king who liked pancakes every morning for breakfast. For lunch he had pancakes, too. For dinner he dined on pancakes. His midnight snacks looked and tasted like pancakes, because that's what they were.

He sent the royal word throughout his kingdom that pancakes were the nation's official food, the only legal food. Everyone was ordered by law to eat pancakes. Pancakes only. Not only that, but people could no longer say "Good morning." They

had to say "Good pancakes." It was even forbidden to say "Thank you." People had to say "Thank pancakes."

Pretty soon the king's subjects were up to their ears in pancakes. So they packed up and left the country. When asked why, they replied, "Who can take all those pancakes?"

The king was sorry about this turn of events. He journeyed to a Good Fairy and asked, "How can I get my people back?"

"Give up pancakes," replied the G.F., "and I'll grant you anything you wish."

"Agreed," agreed the king. "I'll do anything to straighten things out."

"All right," said the Good Fairy, "What, exactly, would you like?"

The king thought for a while, then said, "I'd like some pancakes."

What's the lesson here?

Variety!

Remember to give variety to your voice. That's the lesson

to be learned from the pancake king. He lost his subjects by boring them with too much of a good thing. You need not lose your audience. And you won't lose them—not when you use your secret weapon, variety.

It's a good idea to develop variety with a practice session. The one we will use here is popular in classrooms. Its purpose is to show students just how flexible the human voice can be.

On separate slips of paper the teacher writes the names of various human moods or attitudes. Each student draws a slip of paper and hides behind a screen or door. He then speaks a single sentence using the voice indicated on his slip. For instance, he might speak in a *surprised* tone of voice or talk *sleepily*. The others try to guess just which mood or attitude he is expressing. Some moods will be fairly easy to guess, while others will be more difficult. A good sentence to use is, "My voice tells you how I feel this afternoon." Repeat it once or twice, if necessary.

Here are ten good moods for practice:
1. Surprised
2. Sleepy
3. Excited
4. Tired
5. Puzzled
6. Joyous
7. Bored
8. Sad
9. Disappointed
10. Hopeful.

The poet William Cowper declared, "Variety is the very spice of life, that gives it all its flavour." Well, variety in your voice gives your talk that extra something.

HOW TO WARM UP YOUR VOICE

We've just seen that the human voice is like a fine actor—it can play many rôles. Some, like excitement and hopefulness, make a hit with the people out front. Others, like boredom and sadness, leave an audience cold.

What voice varieties make you a star performer? Let's examine two kinds.

Friendliness wins an audience: Your voice has a personality all its own. That telephone test we told about proves that your voice is *you* to many people. Your voice gives you an opportunity to present a friendly personality toward your audience.

Here is how to tell the difference between a friendly voice and one that lacks warmth. Imagine yourself standing before a group of people. Use a weak, unenthusiastic, flat voice to say, "I like you." It doesn't really sound as if you mean it, does it? Even though the *words* are friendly, the *voice* fails to give them a ring of sincerity. The tone is simply unconvincing. Now speak the very same words with warmth and enthusiasm. Cheerfully exclaim, "I like you!"

See the big difference? That *really* sends the message. It makes your audience glow with pleasure. Your hearers know that you really mean it. Friendliness is like a rubber ball tossed against a wall—it always comes back to you!

Every audience wants warmth and cordiality. Not everyone can give a smashing speech. But anyone can give a kindly one. And it's always better to be kindly.

Use your inspiring voice: What is an inspiring voice? It's a combination of several things. It has the *friendliness* we just talked about. It has *energy*. It's *sincere*. It sounds *self-confident*. It has *dignity* and *poise*.

The way you *sound* depends largely on the way you *feel*. If your emotions are inspired, your voice catches the idea and becomes inspired also. Just as a canary sings brightly when it's happy, your voice sings out when you feel gay.

How can you be sure of having pleasant emotions that give you an inspiring voice? Here are two ways:

1. Prepare your material carefully.
2. Let your material inspire you.

As an example, let me tell you about Mr. Green, a young man who gives talks at a club I sometimes attend. Over the past few months Mr. Green had given several speeches. They were good, but his voice lacked zest and spirit.

One day a miracle happened. Young Mr. Green stood up and gave an especially fascinating talk. It kept us listening every second. He began by telling us that sugar was essential to human life and growth. Then he excitedly informed us how sugar cane grows in tropical climates. After that we learned how sugar beets are cultivated in California.

His voice? It was inspiring! What caused the miraculous change? Because he knew all about sugar, he spoke confidently. (It turned out he had just been hired by a local sugar factory.) He was inspired by his subject—and sounded like it!

If you prepare your subject properly, it will make you sound inspired also!

YOUR VOICE AND YOUR WORDS

Voice and words are partners that can work together to make your talk a good one.

Your voice must pronounce your words clearly—mispronounced words are easily noticed. When you say a difficult word correctly you add dignity to yourself and to your speech. People appreciate the speaker who cares enough to pronounce his words properly.

If you are not sure of a word, look it up in the dictionary. If still puzzled, ask your instructor or parent.

There is no better place to improve pronunciation than in your practice talks. Have someone write down the words that trouble you. Then, look them up. Once you have the right pronunciation, repeat it several times. Say it slowly. Pronounce each syllable separately. Then speak it a bit more swiftly each time. You will soon be in command of the word.

How fast should you talk? A recent television program, just for fun, showed a film that was speeded up ten times beyond normal. Visitors at a zoo zipped from the lions to the monkeys to the elephants in split seconds. It was amusing enough, but entirely too fast for us to make sense. The same with your talk. Too many words crowded into too little time confuses your audience.

Speak just rapidly enough to sound exciting. Speak just slowly enough to be understood. Those two rules will roll your voice along at correct speed. But vary your speed for emphasis.

How loud should you speak? Just loud enough to be heard clearly by people in the back row. This means that sometimes you have to speak louder than at other times, because your voice doesn't carry the same distance in every room. The word *acoustics* is used to describe the sounds in a room or auditorium. The acoustics in a room may carry a speaker's voice, or they may subdue it. Experience will teach you to judge the loudness of your voice.

If you are in doubt, it is perfectly all right to ask the people in the back row whether they can hear you. Professional speakers do this all the time. It shows consideration for the audience. Just remember, if you want your listeners to enjoy you, they must hear you!

Finally, let your voice give emphasis to some of your words. When you come to a strong point, say it strongly. Make it sound as important as it is.

REMINDERS FROM THIS CHAPTER

1. Get acquainted with your voice. That's a good start toward improving it.
2. Remember the importance of your voice when giving a talk.
3. Let your voice describe you as a strong and energetic speaker.
4. Speak with variety. Avoid sameness of tone. Change the rate of speed.
5. Speak with variety in your practice sessions. Notice how many moods your voice can express.
6. Speak with friendly tones.
7. Be inspired by your material. Then, speak out with inspiration!
8. Spend time improving your pronunciation.
9. Speak loud enough to be heard, but avoid shouting.
10. Emphasize words and phrases that deserve emphasis.

Chapter 8

HOW TO LOOK GOOD
TO PEOPLE

A pair of college professors once made an interesting experiment:

They took ten cans of orange juice, all containing the very same brand and quality juice. Bright labels on the cans showed a picture of delicious-looking oranges. The professors then removed the labels from five of the ten cans. One group of five people were given labeled cans to drink, and another group plain, unlabeled cans.

The results of that test were curious. The group drinking from the brightly labeled cans liked the juice much better than the other group. Although the juice was identical in all the cans, the labeled cans received a much higher score. The better the cans looked, the better they liked the contents!

This experiment proved that people are influenced by outward appearance.

This is something we want to remember as public speakers. People like us to *look* good as well as *sound* good. The better you look, the better you sound!

So, in this chapter we are going to take up *personal appearance*. We will discover ways to improve posture, facial expressions, gestures. By the time you finish this chapter you will know how to look good to people.

On a television show the other night a comedian performed a simple but clever act. He spoke to various people as he wandered down the street. He asked a policeman for the time. He told a little girl that her doll was pretty. He talked about the weather with a postman, and so on.

In what way was this clever? Not a single word was spoken! For ten minutes neither the comedian nor the others said anything at all. Yet the audience knew exactly what was going on every second. It was all done in pantomime. The action was made clear by use of body movements, gestures, and facial expressions.

It is amazing how clear you can make yourself by using pantomime gestures for physical actions. A simple nod of the head means *yes*. Hold your palm out to someone and he knows you mean *stop*. A wave means *good-bye*. A hand cupped to your ear indicates that you are *listening*.

When you are talking, act as if your words are not being heard. Employ every appropriate attractive action and pleasant facial expression.

LET YOUR ACTIONS TALK FOR YOU

You speak to your audience before you ever say a single word! How? By the way you walk up to the front and stand. So walk to your speaking position with a lively step, but not a hurried one. Be dignified.

Act confidently, since you know exactly what you are doing. Don't stroll or turn around. Don't wave to your audience unless you are trying to be funny.

Act enthusiastically, as if you have something important to say and are anxious to say it. You *do* have valuable information to give.

Act cheerfully, since you have pleasant words to deliver. Your message *is* enjoyable.

The moments before you begin speaking are like the moments while a rocket is being launched into outer space: The path has been set on the launching pad and the way it is powered determines whether it will be launched on the right course. The way you take your position on the platform, and the confidence you exhibit in your own power, will set the atmosphere for your talk.

Once you have reached your speaking position, pause briefly and look at your audience. Do not speak up the moment you reach the front, as this tends to give an appearance of hurry and nervousness. Stand there calmly for just a moment, then speak your opening words.

As your talk goes along, you may wish to change your speaking position. Do so. It is helpful both to you and your audience to move around somewhat. Sometimes you may want to shift positions simply because it feels more comfortable. Other times you may find a movement necessary in order to make a gesture or to reach an object for display.

Maintain good posture at all times. Stand erect, but not

stiff. Good posture is like a healthy tree: It stands upright, bends when it likes, but always comes back to its normal position.

Here are ten valuable rules for action. Work with them and they will work for you:

1. Move casually, easily, naturally.

2. Don't make a sudden movement when in the middle of stating an important point. This loses the attention of your listeners.

3. Don't move around too much.

4. Don't make unnecessary movements. For instance, if you are standing erect you are not likely to rock back and forth on your feet.

5. Don't gaze down at the floor or up at the ceiling or out of the window. The audience is in front!

6. Maintain good eye contact. Look easily from one member of the audience to another. Do this just as you would look from one friend to another during a conversation.

7. Don't make meaningless or awkward movements.

8. Let your arms hang naturally at your sides when not using them. Notice how professional actors do this.

9. When ending your talk, don't hurry off. Pause very briefly to look at your audience. Then, walk calmly away.

10. Try to become aware of your movements. Notice them. Make an effort to strengthen your weak gestures and make the strong ones stronger!

THE MAGIC OF A SMILE

The story is told of an inventor who carried a large box into the office of a manufacturer, and said, "I have just invented a wonderful new machine."

The manufacturer asked, "What does it do?"

The inventor grinned happily. "It does the work of five men."

"Great!" enthused the manufacturer. "When can you deliver it?"

"Just as soon as I've worked out one little problem."

"And what is the problem?"

"It takes six men to operate it."

That story began the talk of a speaker I heard recently. His purpose was to get his audience into a relaxed and happy mood. And that is just what he did. They listened with enjoyment to his entire talk.

The point is this: You can lead your listeners into the kind of a mood you want them to have. You can make them pleased and relaxed. You can keep them eager to hear what you have to say. You have power to win them over to your ideas. It's done with a smile.

When you smile at the people out there you make them feel

like smiling, too. The science of psychology explains how this works. It tells us that *like attracts like*. You have probably noticed how this works when you meet other people. The gay and enthusiastic person makes *you* feel sunny. And notice how the downcast and gloomy individual spreads his gloom over others.

All this is good news for you as a speaker. You can *create* the cheery kind of an audience you want by acting cheerfully yourself!

You don't have to be comic. Show your audience a relaxed and pleasant face. Let your eyes enjoy the people who have come to hear you. Smile. You don't have to work hard at it, and you need not smile all the time. What you want to avoid is a blank look or a frown. Just let a smile appear naturally and easily whenever it wants to appear. That's the kind that looks good.

HELP YOURSELF WITH GESTURES

Do you know how a magician fools his audience? With gestures, with meaningless gestures. He flings his left hand overhead. It really doesn't mean anything, but we follow it just the same. That's when he slips something over on us with his *right* hand. This is called *distraction*. He distracts our eyes with a pointless gesture. Then he does something else less obvious that seems magical.

This points up the importance of gestures in your talk. An audience notices them. Since any big motion attracts attention, the movements you make with your arms and hands can be turned to profit.

You have often seen a political speaker shake his forefinger or slap the table with his palm. Sharp movements like these emphasize a strong point. They command the audience,

"Listen!" They help listeners to "see" as well as hear a major point. But beware of using too many emphatic gestures! Save them for the special ideas you want to get over with a bang.

A second kind of gesture can be used much more often. Always popular with those out front, it is called a story-telling gesture. That's exactly what it does.

You can experiment with different gestures that tell stories, while practicing alone, or with a mirror, or with classmates. Here's how: When in the schoolroom, you stand before the class. You might select a familiar story, such as *Robin Hood*. Then you act it out with gestures of arms and hands to show everything that is happening. Here are movements that could help you tell the story of *Robin Hood:*

1. Pretend to shoot an arrow.
2. Swing arms out in a welcome.
3. Churn arms as if swimming.
4. Shade eyes with palm as you peer.
5. Reach up as if picking fruit.

Practice this once or twice for yourself. Use as many gestures as you can. During an actual talk you will not want to gesture so often. But you will be acquainted with gestures and can use them later in a natural way to add action to your talk.

EIGHT GOOD REASONS

After a few practice sessions with gestures, a teacher asked her speech class, "What are some good reasons you have found for using correct movements?"

Some of the replies were:

"They help to make your points clear."

"Gestures attract and keep attention."

"They make a speech peppier."

"Movements help the speaker to relax."

"They show friendliness toward an audience."

"Gestures help the speaker to think."

"Movements can tell entertaining stories."

"They make the speaker more attractive."

Here you have eight solid reasons for using the magic of movement. But before we leave the subject, I want to tell you a story:

The manager of a market made plans for selling extra packages of chips and tid-bits over a holiday week-end. He believed that he could sell hundreds of extra packages to customers going on trips and picnics. So he prepared a cardboard figure of a man and set it next to the chips shelf. The cardboard man held out his hand in friendly invitation to pick up the chips. It worked. Dozens of extra packages moved out of the store.

But the manager believed that he could do even better. So the next week-end he attached a small electric motor to the figure. It made the arm move back and forth, as if waving to customers. That *moving* sign caught the attention of everyone passing through the store. And it sold hundreds of extra packages.

That story will help you to remember this vital fact about talking to an audience: *Correct physical movements can uplift your speech just as active wings uplift a sparrow.* They can make the difference between an average talk and one that wins applause.

Good actions make you look good to people!

A SUMMARY OF ATTRACTIVE IDEAS

1. As a speaker, you want to look attractive as well as sound good.
2. Your physical actions and your facial expressions can give you a pleasant appearance.
3. Move with confidence and energy. Act like the expert on the subject that you are!
4. Maintain good posture.
5. Review the ten rules for pleasing physical actions.
6. Smile! That makes your listeners smile, too!
7. Practice gestures before a mirror or with a friend.
8. Develop a few gestures for emphasis.
9. Develop a set of story-telling gestures.
10. Read once more the eight good reasons for moving around correctly.

Chapter 9

YOU CAN BE PERSUASIVE

You probably remember the exciting story of Marco Polo who, in the Middle Ages, travelled overland with his father and uncle from his home in Venice, Italy, through India to China. The Orient was a far-away place of mystery to the people of Marco Polo's time, and this was a daring, adventurous journey.

When Marco returned he told everyone the story of what had happened. He described the many rich treasures and jewels he had seen in India, and the strange spices he had found there. He described how he had been welcomed by the mighty Emperor of China, Kublai Khan. And he told his listeners that the Kublai Khan had appointed him to govern the city of Yangchow, a position that made him not only important but wealthy too.

There was just one thing wrong. The people who listened to Marco's story found it hard to believe. Many thought his adventures were too amazing to be true. So they glanced at each other and shrugged.

Marco tried to think of a way to convince them. Finally, a dramatic plan popped into his mind. He invited his friends and relatives to a great banquet. Marco strode into the room wearing a costly Chinese robe. Then he gave a short talk. Once more he told them of his daring adventures. After that, he took a knife from the table and cut open the hem of his robe. Out tumbled a shower of sparkling riches from China—dazzling diamonds, rubies, emeralds.

That absolutely convinced everyone! This was proof. From that day forward Marco Polo was hailed as the greatest adventurer of his time.

This story about Marco Polo will help you with every talk you give. You see, an audience likes to have facts and proofs. People want to be convinced. They like to know that *you* know what you're talking about!

Talks designed to persuade people to certain actions must present facts. Every day, all over the world, hundreds of speeches-to-persuade are delivered, and audiences are waiting to enjoy smoothly persuasive talks.

USE FACTS TO INFLUENCE YOUR AUDIENCE

What is meant by "a fact"? A fact is a statement that backs up a claim in your talk. It is evidence that your claim is accurate, proof that you are right in what you say. For instance, suppose I say:

"The purchase of Alaska was due to the Western Union Telegraph Company."

I have made an interesting claim. But that is not enough. I must go on from there. You may or may not believe my claim, and I need to supply evidence that the statement is correct. You want me to tell you the *facts* about this to satisfy your curiosity over the point. Maybe this is the first you've heard about this little-known event of history. You want to know *how* Western Union helped to obtain possession of Alaska for the United States. So I back up my statement by presenting the facts:

"At the end of the Civil War in 1865, Western Union wanted to join the United States to Europe with a telegraph wire. The company planned to run the wire across Alaska, which was then owned by Russia, across Asia to the eastern part of Europe. The work was started—but something happened in another part of the world. Cyrus Field successfully laid an undersea cable between the United States and Europe. That was a faster and less expensive connection between the two lands, so the telegraph company halted its work in Alaska.

However, while officials of Western Union had been talking with the Russians they had discovered something of considerable interest. They learned that Russia was willing to sell Alaska. The president of Western Union urged the government of the United States to buy that huge territory. That's what it did.

The purchase was made at the cost of only about two cents an acre. And that's how Western Union helped the United States to own Alaska."

See how these facts prove the statement? There is now no doubt that Western Union played the rôle as stated. Everyone is persuaded that these are the facts, and that your claim makes sense.

The rule is: Back up your important statements with convincing facts. You need not use a story each time. Quite often a short statistic will serve. Let's discover how.

STATISTICS ARE PERSUASIVE

A statistic is a brief fact having numbers in it. Here are some interesting statistics:

1. There are 40,000 different kinds of fish in the world.

2. Light travels at a speed of 186,000 miles per second.

3. On a clear night you can see about 4,000 stars without the aid of a telescope.

4. More than 50% of the flowers in the world are red, or a shade of red.

5. The Panama Canal is 40 miles long from the Pacific to the Atlantic oceans.

6. Watches were invented in the 16th century.

7. Figs are about 48% sugar.

8. Rice is believed to have originated in India approximately 3,000 B.C.

Statistics are easy to obtain from dictionaries and encyclopaedias. They provide a popular way to win an audience over to your way of thinking, for your listeners will credit you with being a careful and accurate speaker. Successful lecturers use

at least a few statistics as they go along. Here is a typical statement from a talk:

"Great inventions have developed in every period of world history."

Now you can back up the point. Just mention a handful of well-known inventions and their dates. You might read from a short prepared list like this:

Invention	Year Invented
Thermometer	1593
Piano	1709
Typewriter	1864
Telephone	1876
Submarine	1891

Don't ever read long lists of statistics. Audiences get tired of hearing too many figures and find them difficult to understand. Statistics are like the pillars of a building: There should be enough to hold up the building, but not so many that they get in the way.

A clever speaker finds ways to dramatize his figures. He often presents them as a picture for his audience to see. For instance a speaker might mention how far his product would stretch if placed end to end, or how high a pile of the product would reach, or else compare the figure to something familiar. For example, in talking about the speed of a missile you might compare it with the speed of a car or a bullet or a plane.

To be a persuasive speaker, do these two things with your statistics:

1. Use them to prove your points.
2. Present them in interesting ways.

HOW TO PRODUCE ACTION

Suppose that the purpose of your talk is to persuade your audience to act.

What do you want them to do?

Buy tickets for Saturday's game?

Vote for your candidate for student leader?

Keep the school grounds clean and attractive?

Whatever your purpose, there are clear ways to get your listeners to act as you suggest. Here are four methods of persuasion:

1. Tell them just what action you want.
2. Show them the rewards of the action.
3. Show them how to act.
4. Urge action at once.

Let's take them up one at a time:

1. TELL THEM JUST WHAT ACTION YOU WANT

An American college boy wrote from Paris to his father:

Dear Dad:
Gue$$ what I need mo$t of all? It'$ not clothe$. It'$ not pencil$. Ye$, you gue$$ed right the fir$t time. Plea$e $end today if po$$ible.

Your $on
Ru$$

That young man let his dad know exactly what he wanted him to do!

Likewise, you should let your listeners know just what course you want them to take. Make it clear. Leave no room for doubts. Suggest it several times during your talk. An audience is led to think about many things while hearing your words. It needs to be reminded of the action you want.

Plant suggestions all along the way, just as a gardener plants seeds. Every so often, entwine into your talk short and simple sentences like these:

"Start your own reading program."
"Read the kind of books you like."
"Read more books."

Your suggestions can be as simple as that. Come right out with it. When are people likely to take action? When they know just *what* action to take!

2. SHOW THEM THE REWARDS OF THE ACTION

Suppose someone walked up and said to you in a nice way, "Please climb the tree in your back yard."

You probably wouldn't do it.

Suppose he then added, "I'd appreciate it if you'd climb that tree."

You still wouldn't do it.

Suppose he then told you, "You'll find a gold coin on one of the branches."

You'd do it. Fast!

This points out a basic truth about human nature: We like our actions to *reward* us in some way. Psychologists have proved that the greater the reward the greater the action. The persuasive speaker shows his listeners how their actions will return a benefit. For instance:

"Book reading is *educational*."
"Cheerfulness attracts *friends*."
"A football game is *fun*."
"Neatness improves personal *appearance*."
"Exercise is *healthful*."

Whenever you ask your listeners to act, show them *why*. Give them good reasons for doing what you suggest. That is how a skillful speaker persuades his audience.

3. SHOW THEM HOW TO ACT

In the year 49 B.C. the armies of Julius Caesar were camped outside the walls of Alexandria, Egypt. Caesar was determined to capture that city. But his troops needed water, so he told his engineers, "Get me some fresh water."

They asked, "How? Egypt is a dry country. How can we get fresh water?"

Caesar told them how. He showed his engineers how to build scientific equipment that used the sun's heat to evaporate salt water from the Mediterranean Sea. Caesar's method was basically the same as that used today by modern engineers. The heated water is turned into steam. The steam is then reduced once more to water, leaving the salt behind.

Let that story remind you *how*. Listeners may want to attend the game you are talking about, but they may have questions like these:

"How do I get tickets?"

"How do I get there?"

"Can I catch the school bus?"

Make it easy for your listeners to act. Answer their questions. Show them how.

4. URGE ACTION AT ONCE

Take a look at newspaper advertisements. Notice how they urge you to ACT NOW! and HURRY! and VISIT US TODAY! There is a good reason. The longer a person puts off doing something, the less likely he is to act.

In Chapter 2 we saw that a talk to persuade people should end with an appeal for action. All through your talk you should fire "persuaders" at your listeners. But at the end you fire away with heavy cannon! Leave them wanting desperately to do the thing you are urging them to do.

POINTS THAT PERSUADE

1. Like Marco Polo, present evidence.
2. Find facts that support your program or idea, and use them to back up your statements.
3. Present statistics in interesting ways.
4. When possible, offer your facts or statistics in the form of a simile or story.

5. Let your listeners know just what action you want them to take.
6. Show them how much they gain by going along with you.
7. Show them how to carry out your suggestions.
8. Urge your audience to act at once.

Chapter 10

HOW TO MAKE PEOPLE LIKE AND ENJOY YOU

After a young lady gave a short talk, several young men from the audience came up to her. "I liked your talk a lot," one of them complimented her.

"Thank you," she replied. "What did you like best about it?"

He thought for a moment, then answered, "I guess what I liked best was *you*."

That turns the spotlight on an important truth: When someone likes *you*, he is also attracted to your *actions*. When *you* are likable, so is what you *say*. This is true not only when making a speech, but in every department of living.

A talk contains something more than words, gestures, pleasant facial expressions, and illustrative stories.

It reflects your *personality*.

What is meant by *personality?* It's the collection of personal traits that make up that person called *you*. The way you think and talk, your habits and feelings and opinions, your actions and your facial expressions are included. Just as a whole tree is made up of blossoms and branches and roots, so is each person made up of various characteristics.

Can a person's personality become brighter? Certainly! Life offers everyone the opportunity to make himself into a better person.

As your personality grows, so does that magic touch called

flexibility, meaning adaptability to a situation. If you feel that your audience is *with* you and enjoying your talk, you can suddenly switch from a serious mood to a humorous one. A speaker from the telephone company, for example, was telling his audience how to speak correctly on the phone. In the middle of a series of suggestions he suddenly said, "The other day we had a call from a lady with a problem. 'My phone cord is too long,' she told us. 'Will you please pull it back at your end?'"

Speaking to an audience helps develop your personality. Then, the more your personality sparkles, the better speaker you become. So, you see, everything spirals upwards when you speak!

WHAT MAKES YOUR PERSONALITY ATTRACTIVE?

What makes you an interesting and appreciated person when you stand before an audience? The simple truth is, there is nothing in the world finer than old-fashioned character traits. I want to list fifteen of them for your examination. Look them over. Notice that you naturally like to be around people who possess these traits:

1. Courage	9. Patience
2. Helpfulness	10. Effort
3. Encouragement	11. Promptness
4. Open-mindedness	12. Friendliness
5. Reliability	13. Simplicity
6. Calmness	14. Accuracy
7. Modesty	15. Self-responsibility
8. Tact	

More and more you can add these rich qualities to your

platform appearances. They make you a finer speaker. They give extra glow to your personality.

Take, for example, that admirable character trait we call *courage*. Do you know who the courageous man really is?

He's the man *willing to go ahead with what he's a bit timid about doing*. Like giving his first few talks. The courageous and heroic person says to himself, "This may be new and frightening, but I'll do it!"

That's courage.

And that's what your audience appreciates. The people out front don't expect you to give perfect talks. All they expect you to do is *try*.

Some years ago a young salesman had several dozen watches, but no customers for them. He decided to try something new— he would try to sell the watches through the mails. So he wrote to people in nearby towns, telling them of his fine watches. They bought every one! That young man succeeded because he tried. His name was Richard W. Sears, and he was the founder of what is today the world's largest mail order company.

Let's look at another personality trait, that of *helpfulness*. How does that make you a better speaker? When you make a point clearer with a story, and get your audience to understand a new idea, you are being helpful to your audience, and this will be appreciated.

One of the best-loved books of all time was written because its author had an *encouraging* personality. One day a 12-year-old boy named Lloyd Osbourne was unhappy. It was a holiday, but it was raining too hard for him to go out and play. So Lloyd's stepfather started telling him an adventure story. It was all about bold pirates and buried treasure. Out of that rainy-day story came the book *Treasure Island*. It was written by Lloyd's stepfather, Robert Louis Stevenson.

Someone once said, "The best way to be liked is to be likable." That's quite an idea, come to think of it.

SPEAK WITH ENTHUSIASM

Have you noticed how quickly we are attracted by the enthusiastic personality? We like to be near such a person. He makes *us* feel energetic. Ralph Waldo Emerson, the famous American author, once declared, "Enthusiasm is the leaping lightning." Just as a flash of lightning brightens the sky, the enthusiastic personality brightens our lives.

What is the secret here? When *you* are energetic, you make your audience that way, too. It's something like the game of Follow the Leader. As you speak with energy, your audience happily follows your lead.

Remember, your listeners really *want* to get excited over your talk. You can arouse their enthusiasm by being enthusiastic yourself!

One young man gave a classroom talk about life in ancient Egypt. It was a good talk, for it included some interesting facts about the Nile River. But it just wasn't an enthusiastic speech. The young speaker was not very excited about the ancient Egyptians, so he decided to choose his next topic by looking in the library for something that really interested him. In wandering through the bookshelves he discovered the story of a young clerk named George Eastman. He read that this clerk was once about to take a trip when a friend gave him a suggestion: Take some photographs of the journey. In those days photography was a new and untested adventure, but the young clerk decided to experiment with it. That chance suggestion started Eastman on the road to fame. He became a skilled inventor and finally established the photographic company that bears his name.

Eastman's was an exciting story that really interested the speaker. So he turned it into a talk—an enthusiastic one!

It is always a good idea to select topics of interest to you personally. Don't think that others won't be interested in them. It has been said that there are no dull subjects; there are only speakers who fail to make them exciting. I was once part of an audience listening to a talk about honeybees. Few of us knew much about them, but that speaker made honeybees just about the most fascinating little creatures on earth. Among many things, he told us that a honeybee really works hard. It never sleeps and it flies a distance equal to two trips around the world, just to gather a single pound of honey! At the end of his talk he was surrounded by guests who wanted to know more about honeybees.

Be an enthusiastic personality. That's how you create enthusiastic audiences!

BE SUCCESS-MINDED

Read the following story which won first prize in a speaking contest:

"One day a young man named George Westinghouse was travelling by train. He was on his way to the city of Troy, in New York. Suddenly, the train came to a jolting stop. The conductor explained to the young man 'There's a wreck on the tracks ahead. We had to make that quick stop to avoid a collision. It shakes up passengers, but there's no way to bring a train to a slow and easy stop.'

"In those days trains were stopped by hand brakes. Each car had a brake that had to be turned at least a half mile before the intended stop.

"Young George Westinghouse wondered whether he might improve things. Better brakes for a train was an exciting challenge. He plunged into action. Late at night he could be

seen bent over drawings. Still later, during those nights, he could be found testing and experimenting with brakes. Finally, he came up with an answer: *Compressed air could bring a speeding train to a swift and smooth stop!*

"George Westinghouse thought he had succeeded—but there were hurdles ahead. The idea was good all right, but the railway companies he called upon weren't convinced. The young man saw that he had to be a salesman as well as an inventor. He tackled that challenge, too. He gave informative and interesting talks about his new invention.

"That did it! A railway company agreed to test the air brakes. They worked! Young George Westinghouse was on his way to fame and fortune."

That story was told by a success-minded speaker. He told it well because it was a success story and he was success-minded.

What is meant by being "success-minded"? You simply believe firmly that success is possible. You prove that problems can be tackled and solved.

Success-minded speakers are always in demand. Be one!

THE MOST VALUABLE PERSON OF ALL

A hundred university students were once asked. "What do you want most from other people?"

Some needed loyalty. Others wanted someone to encourage them. Still others liked to share company with cheerful and pleasant people. There were many other answers, too. But when everything was added up, do you know what everyone wanted most of all?

Understanding.

The majority of students wanted to be understood more and

criticized less. The most valuable kind of friend in the entire world is the one who quietly understands you! When you understand someone you cheerfully accept him just the way he is, and give him your patience and kindness. You are being an understanding personality when you simply like and enjoy another's company.

How can you be an understanding speaker? You are already on your way! Many of the ideas in previous pages have helped you to understand your audiences. For instance, you know already that your listeners want you to be friendly and energetic and encouraging.

In addition, your audience seeks *human interest* or empathy. What exactly does that mean? Human interest means simply talking about things of interest to humans! It can be a friendly remark tossed suddenly to your listeners. Or it can be a light touch, a quip, a pun. You excite human interest when you talk about popular subjects, such as entertainment, travel, food, cars or family. One high school speaker delighted his audience with this human-interest remark, "I gave my dad the shock of his life last Saturday. I asked him for the garage keys and came out with the lawn mower."

The word *empathy* means the ability to enter into the thoughts and feelings of another person. It means just about the same thing as *understanding*. But you can call it by either word you want. Just develop it. It develops your personality!

SPECIAL IDEAS FROM THIS CHAPTER

1. Your personality is an important feature of your talk.
2. Anyone can build a brighter and stronger personality. That includes you.
3. Speaking before an audience helps you develop likable personality traits.

4. Review the fifteen character traits listed in this chapter. Apply them to your talks.
5. You don't have to be perfect. You *do* have to try.
6. Be a helpful and encouraging speaker.
7. Remember the magic of enthusiasm. It turns average talks into exciting ones!
8. Be success-minded, be a successful speaker.
9. Put yourself in the place of your audience. Understand what they need from you as a speaker.
10. Spice your talk with human interest items.

Chapter 11

QUESTION-AND-ANSWER SESSION

To ask questions is one of the finest ways to gain knowledge. It has always been a popular and intelligent method for enriching yourself. However, half of the job is putting the answer to work for you!

A young man, about to give a speech, asked his instructor, "What are the most beautiful words in the English language?"

"That's a matter of personal opinion," was the reply. "However, I can name ten words which most people believe to be among the most beautiful." The teacher then named them.

The young speaker noted them carefully, then stood before his audience and said, "Ladies and gentlemen, *melody, love, joy, liberty, adoration, hope, modesty, sympathy, faith, happiness*," and sat down abruptly.

His teacher asked, surprised, "What kind of a talk was that?"

"That," came the reply, "was a beautiful talk!"

The young man had asked a good question all right, but he applied the answer incorrectly. You can do much better! In this chapter, we will pose some important questions, answer them and help you to apply the answers.

FASCINATING FACTS

"How can I keep my audience interested in my talk?"

In this book we have covered several lively ways to keep your listeners listening, but here's an extra tip: Use *fascinating facts*. There are many short bits of curious information that catch attention. Here are some examples:

1. Columbus was paid the sum of $320 for discovering America.

2. The cantaloupe is named after the city of Cantaloupe in Italy, where it was first grown.

3. The third brightest object in the sky, after the Sun and Moon, is the planet Venus.

4. Sir Arthur Conan Doyle, author of the famous detective stories about Sherlock Holmes, named that great detective after an American writer. Doyle chose the name after reading the works of Oliver Wendell Holmes.

5. The ten most often used words in the English language are *the, of, and, to, in, a, is, that, be, it.*

6. The giant dinosaurs who lived millions of years ago in the United States were often more than 85 feet in length.

7. The Amazon River in South America is 150 miles wide at the point where it reaches the ocean.

8. The cheetah is the swiftest animal in the world. It speeds along at 70 miles per hour.

9. The Japanese have a clever system for scattering flower seeds around their country. They tie packets of seeds to balloons and send them soaring.

10. There are stars with larger diameters than the distance between Earth and Sun (93,000,000 miles).

11. The month of June is named after an ancient Roman family named Junius.

12. The sweet potato was introduced to Europe by Spanish explorers who discovered it in the West Indies.

Audiences are attracted to curious bits of information like these. Just as a good cook spices her cake to make it tastier, you can add spice to your talk by mixing in a few fascinating facts.

CONCENTRATE ON EACH PART

"How can I prepare and deliver my talk the easiest way?"

This is an excellent question. And it has a simple answer: concentrate on one thing at a time.

You are acting wisely when you do things as simply as possible. This is a major secret of success in everything you do, whether in giving a talk or anything else.

How exactly does one proceed as simply as possible? In Chapter 3 you saw that *concentration* helps your home practice. Apply this idea to each part of your talk in turn. For a reasonable length of time, throw all your energies into one area.

When working on the ending, forget everything else and concentrate on the ending. If you are building self-confidence, give it your full attention.

Concentrate on one thing at a time, and do it well. This sort of simplification will make your speaking more powerful.

QUESTION SESSION

"When should I answer questions from the audience?"

At certain types of meeting it is a good idea to tell your listeners before you begin that you will open the meeting to questions from the audience at the conclusion of your talk. Your listeners will look forward to taking an active part in the talk, enjoy asking specific questions about your points. A relaxed question-and-answer period will probably result in lots of fun and enlightenment, for you as well.

To get into this discussion period, end your talk something like this: "Now, if you have questions about anything we've covered, we can go into them at this time." Some listeners want to ask questions but are shy about raising their hands. So give them a word or two of friendly encouragement. Recently I heard a lecturer do it with this remark: "Remember, Columbus once asked whether the world was round or not. Your questions will probably be simpler to answer."

One teacher uses question-and-answer sessions to help train speakers think quickly on their feet. The practice goes like this: A student talks for about one minute on a subject he knows expertly. Then the meeting is opened to questions. The audience fires them one after another. The speaker shoots back his answers as swiftly and as calmly as he can. This builds a speaker's self-command before an audience. This method is also excellent for practicing at home with a friend or two.

ALL ABOUT QUOTATIONS

"Why do speakers quote the words of famous people? How can I use quotations in my talk?"

The words of other people can add value to your own statements. By quoting another person you serve your listeners with that man's wisdom. An audience likes to hear appropriate ideas that a famous authority has to say about your subject. When someone like Abraham Lincoln or Benjamin Franklin agrees with you—that's something!

Benjamin Disraeli, the great Prime Minister of England, declared, "The wisdom of the wise and the experience of the ages may be preserved by quotation."

There is a quotation on practically every subject. Some quotations are serious, others funny. Many point out helpful lessons. Some offer encouragement. But almost all have their place.

Here are a few comments made by famous people:

1. Benjamin Franklin: "Remember that time is money."

2. Thomas Carlyle: "There is always hope in a man who actually and earnestly works."

3. Ralph Waldo Emerson: "Books are the best of things, if well used."

4. Marcus Aurelius: "Our life is what our thoughts make it."

5. Washington Irving: "A kind heart is a fountain of gladness, making everything in its vicinity freshen into smiles."

Keep your quotations brief. Do not use too many in a short talk, and don't run them together. Choose apt quotations and be sure you tell your audience the name of the person quoted.

Libraries have books filled with nothing but excellent quotations. You will find plenty to illustrate your talk.

NOTES OR NOT?

"Please comment on the use of notes. When should they be used?"

Notes are only to aid the memory. In classroom talks, your teacher will instruct you whether or not to use notes. If you need them, use them. If you can speak without notes, fine. As you give more and more talks, use fewer and fewer notes. This builds your ability to speak up in a free and easy way.

Your notes can be written out in any way that helps you. One speaker might write down the single key-word *Parrot*. This reminds him to tell the audience how parrots are trained to talk. Another speaker might write out a complete key-sentence, like, *Three benefits of learning to swim* to guide him into telling of several values of swimming.

Write your notes on cards about 3 × 5 inches. Use one side only. Number the cards. Write the reminders large enough to be read at a glance. Do not handle notes unnecessarily, and turn them quietly while you are speaking.

A cartoon once showed a fox who was determined to build his muscles. He practiced by jumping across a stream. At first he helped himself by leaping from rock to rock in the water. One day the helpful rocks disappeared. But he was a courageous fox, so he jumped without them, and made it!

Be like that fox. Use notes until you can speak without them.

HAVE A GOOD TIME

"How long should a speech be?"

There's a popular riddle that asks, "How long should a dog's legs be?" The answer is, "Long enough to reach the ground."

That's good advice when it comes to talking, too. You should

speak just long enough to cover your subject. Of course, if you have been given a definite time limit, such as five minutes, plan for five minutes. In preparing your speech, practice until you are sure that your five minutes will allow you to cover the topic as fully as possible.

Do not go beyond the time limit either. Let your talk be timed by the clock—not by the calendar! Also, watch the time during your speech. If you are not sure how long you have left to speak, ask whoever is in charge of the program. This is a wise and courteous question on your part.

Good timing comes with practice and experience. Many teachers help their students by this method: Thirty seconds before the speaker's time is up, the teacher sounds a signal, by ringing a bell quietly, or tapping a pencil on a desk. This reminds you to start wrapping things up. After a while you will develop a sense of timing so that a signal is unnecessary. Your talk need not stop on the exact second. Just try to end it within about thirty seconds.

You can also practice timing at home. Set an alarm clock but keep it in sight, so you can watch the minutes as you talk. Glance at the time every once in a while to see how you are coming, and lengthen or shorten your speech accordingly.

Remember, it's the quality of a talk that counts, not its quantity. The most famous example of this happened at the town of Gettysburg, Pennsylvania, on November 19, 1863. A mighty battle of the Civil War had recently been fought at Gettysburg. Leading members of the United States government were gathered to pay homage to the soldiers who had died. A famous orator named Edward Everett gave a speech lasting for two hours. Then, President Lincoln rose to speak. His talk lasted for only five minutes. It was a simple and sincere speech, it said what needed to be said, and that was all.

REVIEW OF QUESTIONS AND ANSWERS

1. Serve your listeners fascinating facts.
2. Simplify everything about your talk. Make it easy on yourself.
3. If possible and time allows, have a question-and-answer period at the end of your talk.

4. Practice with questions and answers, as outlined in this chapter.
5. Quote famous people. Add their wisdom to your talk.
6. Use notes when necessary, but practice speaking without them, too.
7. Keep within the time limits of your talk.
8. Pack as much interesting information as possible into your allotted time.

Chapter 12

SPECIAL PLANS
FOR PRIZE-WINNING TALKS

A small boy had his picture taken while standing alongside the Grand Canyon in Arizona. When asked what he liked best in the picture he replied, "I like to see myself in it."

That boy brings us to our first special plan for prize-winning talks. Anyone who talks before an audience should keep it in mind constantly:

Include your audience in your talk.

Your listeners not only want to hear your speech, but they like to get themselves into it. They want to take a personal part in whatever is being said. Psychologists call this the need for personal participation. Quite often the difference between a dull speaker and an exciting one is that the exciting one remembers this.

How can you include your audience in your talk?

VISUAL DISPLAY

One of the best ways is to use visual aids. Display an object connected with your topic. This lets people *see* as well as *hear*. No matter what your subject may be, you can always associate some kind of visual object with it. I have seen three recent speakers use the following displays:

An artist who told us about using paints in artwork set several fruits and vegetables on a table. He held them up one at a time to show how nature painted the apple red and the squash yellow.

A chief of police lecturing on traffic safety set up a large map of the countryside. He moved miniature cars along the highways to illustrate safe driving.

A young lady from a large baking company displayed dozens of strawberry cup-cakes. At the end of the talk she passed them around!

You don't need large or complicated objects. Even such simple things as a book or hat can be associated with your talk.

Another good method for inviting your audience into your talk is to refer to familiar experiences they have had. You might ask your listeners, "Do you remember the movie we saw in this auditorium last week?" The instant you mention that movie your listeners go into mental action, for they know exactly what you are talking about. You could then go on to use that movie to make a point.

Remember, a successful talk is like a ball game with you throwing the ball. You toss ideas and anecdotes to your audience. They take mental swings at them. That makes an exciting game for everyone!

ACTION!

Do you know the kind of television program people like best? Not a Western. Not a romance. Not a mystery.

A story with *action*!

It might have a cowboy background or a romantic theme, but the most popular is the drama that rolls along with exciting action, has something happening all the time. You know how it goes: In one scene the police race through town, sirens whining.

Next, they are battling it out with the bandits. Finally, they rescue the beautiful heroine. That's the kind of excitement we like.

A talk before an audience is a lot like that. Your listeners want exciting things to happen most of the time. This is a great opportunity for you to be a popular speaker through *action*. This doesn't mean that you need to turn handsprings or anything like that. It just means that you propel your talk forward by using attractive methods. Here are just a few examples:

Excite the imagination: Your listeners' imagination wants to build mental pictures. Picture yourself standing in front of the White House as the President comes out. Next, imagine that you are stretched out comfortably on the soft sands of a beautiful island of the South Seas. Finally, see yourself walking around on the surface of the moon.

You can get your audience into imaginative action by saying, "Let your imagination fly you away to the moon." Then, let them imagine the scene as you describe it.

Mention well-known items: Your audience likes to hear of famous people. Their ears bend your way when you mention familiar places and products.

Change the scenery of your talk: A holiday trip stays exciting as the view shifts from mountains to desert to seashore. So be sure to use anecdotes to change the scenery of your talk. Recently I heard a speaker cover the topic of *opportunity*. After advising his audience to make the most of every opportunity he changed the scenery with an anecdote. He told of a cowboy named Jim White who was riding the range in New Mexico one afternoon. Off in the distance he saw what appeared to be a thick column of smoke rising out of the ground. To Jim White, it looked like an opportunity for adventure, so he rode over to the spot. What he had thought was smoke turned out to be something entirely different. It was an army of bats flying out of a deep cave. That was how Jim White discovered the famous Carlsbad Caverns.

These are types of actions that keep your listeners excited—and listening! Of course you won't want to include too many in a short talk. Just become acquainted with a few and use them wherever you can. After a while you will find yourself reaching for them in a natural way, just as you reach out to pick a ripe fruit from a branch.

SPEECH CHART

The story is told about Tom and Eddie who were walking down the street. Tom stopped at a phone booth and told Eddie, "Wait a second. I'm going to phone a grocery market

about a job." When Tom dialed a number, Eddie heard the following conversation:

"Hello, Mr. Miller. How is your new clerk doing? I see—he's doing just fine. Is he a good worker? I'm glad to hear he is. Well, good-by, Mr. Miller."

As Tom hung up, Eddie sympathized, "Too bad you didn't get hired."

"Oh," Tom cheerfully replied, "I was hired a week ago. I was just checking up on myself."

You will make faster progress if you—like Tom—check up on yourself as you go along. Even the best of speakers review their platform appearances so as to improve them.

Use the following *Speech Chart* to check on yourself during your classroom talks or in practice sessions at home. Here is how: Copy the chart on a sheet of paper. Write your name in the blank space provided. Then give the chart to someone who will check you—either the teacher or another student. The fifteen items are among the most important covered in this book. The five blank spaces, from 16 to 20, can be filled in with additional items that you or the instructor may wish checked.

The person checking scores each item with a *3, 2,* or *1*. A *3* means *good;* *2* indicates *fair;* and *1* means that you should *concentrate on improving* this item especially. The sample chart is filled out to give you an idea of scoring.

The Speech Chart idea is excellent too for a contest. The winner is the person with the greatest number of total points.

The most important thing to remember about the chart is its purpose. The whole idea is to let it be *helpful.* When you are the checker, score the speaker in the way that helps him the most. When you are being checked, let the score on the different items point out where you can be an even better speaker!

SPEECH CHART

Speaker's name ....

Items	Points
1. Enthusiasm	2
2. Posture	3
3. Use of anecdotes	1
4. Picturesque words	2
5. Self-confidence	2
6. Correct gestures	3
7. Voice	1
8. Appealing personality	3
9. Simplicity	2
10. Dramatic sense	3
11. Facial expressions	2
12. Action	2
13. Clearness of ideas	1
14. Persuasiveness	2
15. General interest	3
16.	
17.	
18.	
19.	
20.	

HOW TO IMPROVE YOURSELF QUICKLY!

A book salesman told a young lady, "Miss, read this book and you'll be a genius in just four weeks."

"Better sell me two copies," she eagerly answered, "I'm taking a test in two weeks."

That's not quite the way to learn quickly, but there *are* techniques that can speed you up. Let's talk about five of them.

Explore this book constantly: There was once a prospector who went exploring for gold in a mountain. On his first trip he found only the mountain. The next time he discovered a valley in the mountain. On his third trip he found a cave in the valley in the mountain. On his fourth journey he discovered gold in the cave in the valley in the mountain.

That's how it can be with you and this book. Explore it constantly. Each time you will make more valuable discoveries. Keep notes on the ideas that you find especially helpful. Review those ideas, concentrate on them. Practice. Apply all improvements to your talks. That is how to find the kind of gold that makes your speeches rich!

Work with your teacher: Let your instructor give you help. He or she can offer you the benefit of valuable experience. Hundreds of years ago a Roman writer named Plautus said, "Every man needs the advice of some wise friend in the affairs of life." Giving a talk is an affair where good advice is always needed!

Have confidence in your talents: A few weeks ago I saw a submarine break through the surface of the sea. For a few moments there was nothing on deck except the salt water washing down the sides of the ship. Then, suddenly, the hatch flew open. Up popped a dozen sailors who raced to their duties all over the deck.

Psychologists tell us that we are somewhat like that submarine. All of us have hidden talents and energies. We need only release them through preparations and practice. Then we find ourselves popping up with all sorts of delightful talents. Now that you know this, have lots of confidence in yourself.

Challenge yourself: Challenge yourself to do a bit better each time you give a talk. A self-challenge is profitable and it is fun. One of the most famous paintings in the world was created by a challenge. It happened when two noted artists had a lively discussion. The famous men were Sir Joshua Reynolds and Thomas Gainsborough. Reynolds told Gainsborough that blue was not suitable as the main theme of a painting. Gainsborough insisted that it was. Gainsborough then challenged himself to prove his point. The result? He painted one of the best-known pictures in the world, *The Blue Boy.*

Something to remember: Finally, I'd like you to remember an exciting plan. It's one we covered at the very start of this book. This plan gives you a better speech and it makes you a happier speaker. You will win both of these rich rewards if you will:
Enjoy yourself!

PRIZE-WINNING POINTS TO REVIEW

1. Include your audience in your talk. From time to time, invite your listeners to take an active part.
2. Load your speech with action!
3. Excite the imagination of the people out front.
4. Change the scenery of your talk. Give your listeners variety.
5. Use the *Speech Chart.* Let it aid both your classroom sessions and your practice at home.
6. Keep in mind the fifteen items of the *Speech Chart.* They help build prize-winning talks.
7. Use this book constantly. Let it guide you.
8. Get help and advice from your instructor. Ask questions.
9. Keep your self-confidence sky-high.
10. Whenever you prepare or deliver a talk—enjoy yourself!

INDEX

Action, 115
    produce, 91
    show rewards of, 92
    urge, 94
    you want, 92
Actions talk for you, 79
All about quotations, 109
Anecdotes from history, 53
    provide entertainment, 52
    shed light, 51
    ways to use, 50
Audience, take command of, 43
    use facts to influence, 88

Bang, start with, 24
Be a natural speaker, 41
    persuasive, 86
    success-minded, 101
Build positive attitudes, 45

Chart, speech, 117
Choose a topic, 14
Classroom plan, 46
    practice is valuable, 36
Concentrate on each part, 107

Display, visual, 114

Eight good reasons, 83
End your talk, how to, 27
Entertainment, anecdotes provide, 52
Enthusiasm, speak with, 99
Experiences, tell your, 54

Facts, fascinating, 106
    use, 88
Friend, practice with, 34

Gain courage, self-confidence, 40
Gestures, help with, 82
Giving exciting talk, 49
Good time, have, 110

Have a good time, 110
Help yourself, how to, 31
    yourself with gestures, 82
Helpful points for your review, 57
History, anecdotes from, 53
Hit, positive words make, 60

How others succeed, 37
    to act, 93
    to build positive attitudes, 45
    to choose a topic, 14
    to end your talk, 27
    to gain courage and self-confidence, 40
    to help yourself, 31
    to improve yourself quickly, 119
    to look good to people, 77
    to make people like and enjoy you, 96
    to prepare your talk the easy way, 20
    to produce action, 91
    to warm up your voice, 72

Ideas, special, 103
    summary of attractive, 85
Important ideas to remember, 28
Improve yourself quickly, 119

Jokes and stories, use, 55

Keep in mind, thoughts to, 39

Let anecdotes provide entertainment, 52
    anecdotes shed light on your points, 51
    your actions talk for you, 79
    your words work for you, 59
Local stories are popular, 56
Look good to people, 77

Magic of a smile, 81
Make people like and enjoy you, 96
    your words descriptive, 63
Middle is the strongest section, 26
Most valuable person of all, 102

Notes or not, 110

Paint a word-picture, 64
Part, concentrate on each, 107
People like you, make, 96
    look good to, 77
Person, most valuable, 102
Personality, attractive, 97

Persuade, points that, 94
Plan, classroom, 46
Plans, summary of helpful, 48
Points, anecdotes shed light on, 51
    for your review, 57
    prize-winning, 121
    that persuade, 94
    valuable, 19
Positive words make a hit, 60
Practice is valuable, classroom, 36
    with a friend or two, 34
Prepare your talk the easy way, 20
Prize-winning points to review, 121
    talks, 114
Produce action, how to, 91
Purpose, what is your, 16

Question-and-answer session, 105
Questions and answers, review of, 112
Question session, 108
Quotations, all about, 109

Reasons, eight good, 83
Remember about words, 67
Review of questions and answers, 112
    points for, 57
Rewards of action, 92
Rule, start with, 13

Secrets for giving an exciting talk, 49
Section, middle is strongest, 26
Show them how to act, 93
    them the rewards of the action, 92
Smile, magic of, 81
Speak with enthusiasm, 99
Speaker, be a natural, 41
Special ideas from this chapter, 103
    plans for prize-winning talks, 114
Speech chart, 117, 119
Start with this delightful rule, 13
Statistics are persuasive, 89
Stories are popular, local, 56
    use jokes and, 55
Strongest section, 26
Succeed, how others, 37
Success-minded, be, 101
Summary of attractive ideas, 85
    of helpful plans, 48

Take complete command of your
    audience, 43

Talk, giving exciting, 49
Talks make you valuable, 12
    prize-winning, 114
Tell of your own experiences, 54
    them just what action you
    want, 92
Thoughts to keep in mind, 39
Titles wanted, exciting, 17
Topic, how to choose, 14
Two ways to use anecdotes, 50

Urge action at once, 94
Use anecdotes, 50
    clear words, 62
    facts to influence your audience,
    88
    jokes and humorous stories, 55

Valuable points from this chapter, 19
Vary your voice, 69
Visual display, 114
Vocabulary is treasure, 66
Voice and words, 74
    make you attractive, 68
    vary your, 69
    warm up your, 72

Wanted: exciting titles, 17
Warm up your voice, 72
Ways to use anecdotes, 50
What is your purpose, 16
    makes your personality attractive,
    97
    to remember about words, 67
Word-picture, paint, 64
Words descriptive, make, 63
    use clear, 62
    voice and, 74
    what to remember, 67
    work for you, 59

You can be persuasive, 86
    make people like, 96
    will enjoy talking to an audience,
    11
Your talk, end, 27
    talk, prepare the easy way, 20
    talks make you more valuable, 12
    vocabulary is your treasure, 66
    voice and your words, 74
    voice can make you attractive, 68

NOTES

NOTES